100
Barbecue Dishes

100
Barbecue Dishes

Edited by
Gill McCormick

HAMLYN

Contents

NOTES
Standard spoon measurements are used in all recipes
1 tablespoon = one 15 ml spoon
1 teaspoon = one 5 ml spoon
All spoon measures are level.
Where amounts of salt and pepper are not specified, the cook should use her own discretion.
Canned foods should not be drained, unless so stated in the recipe.
For all recipes, quantities are given in metric, imperial and American measures. Follow one set of measures only, because they are not interchangeable.

First published in 1984 by
Octopus Books Limited

This edition published in 1991 by
The Hamlyn Publishing Group Limited,
part of Reed International Books,
Michelin House, 81 Fulham Road,
London SW3 6RB

ISBN 0 600 57243 9

Produced by Mandarin Offset
Printed and bound in Hong Kong

Frontispiece: A Garden Barbecue
(Photograph: New Zealand Lamb Information Bureau)

Introduction

Barbecues are great fun for all the family and a marvellous way of entertaining friends at home. Nothing will whet your guests' appetites more than the delicious aroma of food cooking over charcoal.

Eating out in the garden can be enjoyed all the year round. Sizzling sausages and foil-wrapped baked potatoes are just as good at a chilly November fireworks party as kebabs, salads and long cool drinks on a hot summer's day.

Almost any food you can cook in an oven or under a grill can be barbecued, and will taste all the better for the spicy sauces, marinades and bastes which traditionally accompany barbecued foods.

This book provides all the ingredients for relaxed entertaining. Recipes cover the four main methods of barbecue cooking – open grilling, cooking in foil, spit roasting and kebab cooking – and there are appetizers, accompaniments and desserts too.

Setting up and lighting your barbecue

There are plenty of purpose-built barbecues available in the shops or you can quite easily build your own with fire-bricks. To make your own barbecue stand, simply build two walls about 45 cm (18 inches) apart on an earth or concrete base. Line the floor with foil, then make a flat bed of charcoal on top of paper and dry sticks. Place the grill on top, allowing at least 10 cm (4 inches) between the top of the charcoal and the rack.

The size of your barbecue depends on how many you regularly cook for. As a rough guide, an area of approximately 45 cm (18 inches) square gives sufficient space to cook for eight people.

Charcoal chips or briquettes are the traditional fuel for barbecues. Do not under any circumstances use branded firelighters or dangerous liquids such as paraffin or petrol as they can taint the food and, more importantly, flare up and lead to nasty accidents. Special solid fuel tablets are available from chemists and are an efficient way of getting the fire going.

Timing is all important. Charcoal chips generally need to burn for 45 minutes to an hour before they are hot enough for cooking. Briquettes are much faster and will be ready in 30 to 40 minutes.

When lighting the fire, push the coals into a pyramid shape to allow the air to circulate. The coals are ready when they are burning grey with a red glow. Spread them out and, if necessary, sprinkle the surface with more charcoal.

The cooking heat can be varied by adjusting the distance between the food and the hottest part of the fire, the centre. Large items of food should be placed in the centre and small ones around it.

What you will need

Basic utensils are all you need for barbecue cooking. Make sure you have a long-handled fork, spoon and fish slice – and tongs for the coal. A small paint brush is the best way of basting the food and a container filled with warm water is handy for damping down the flames which occasionally flare up.

Aluminium foil is useful for wrapping certain foods. Foil wrapped foods can be placed directly in the coals or on the grill above. A hinged wire tray is useful for foods which may break easily, such as hamburgers or fish, and skewers are essential for testing foods and for cooking kebabs.

A good-quality oven mit, a damp cloth and a roll of kitchen paper are all useful, together with a table placed beside the barbecue on which you can place the food and marinades.

Appetizers

Start your next barbecue party with one or two delicious appetizers. Eating outdoors encourages hearty appetites and your guests will appreciate something to eat while the food is cooking.

Citrus and Melon Cocktail

METRIC/IMPERIAL	AMERICAN
2 oranges, peeled, segmented and chopped	2 oranges, peeled, segmented and chopped
1 grapefruit, peeled, segmented and chopped	1 grapefruit, peeled, segmented and chopped
1 melon, peeled and chopped	1 melon, peeled, and chopped
2 tablespoons mayonnaise	2 tablespoons mayonnaise
mint to garnish	mint to garnish

In a large bowl, mix the oranges, grapefruit and melon and stir in the mayonnaise.

Chill before serving in individual glass dishes, garnished with the mint.
Serves 4

Egg Mayonnaise

METRIC/IMPERIAL	AMERICAN
1 small lettuce	1 small head lettuce
4 hard-boiled eggs	4 hard-cooked eggs
6 tablespoons mayonnaise	6 tablespoons mayonnaise
3 tablespoons milk	3 tablespoons milk
1–2 teaspoons paprika	1–2 teaspoons mild paprika

Place the lettuce on a serving dish or on individual plates. Cut the eggs in half lengthwise and arrange, cut side down, on top of the lettuce. Mix the mayonnaise and milk in a small bowl and pour over the eggs.

Sprinkle with paprika to taste.
Serves 4

Egg Mayonnaise, Avocado and Prawn, Citrus and Melon Cocktail, a dish of Quick Appetizers (Photograph: Hellmann's Real Mayonnaise)

Quick Appetizers

1. Add chopped herbs, garlic or cream cheese to mayonnaise and use as a spread for small slices of melba toast.
   This mixture will pipe if well chilled.
2. Mix together flaked canned fish – tuna, salmon or sardines – and cream cheese or mayonnaise and use to stuff small button mushrooms, wedges of cucumber or pieces of crispy celery.
   Garnish with slices of lemon and small sprigs of parsley.
3. Stir cooked, diced meat and a colourful vegetable or fruit into mayonnaise and use as a quick filling for vol-au-vents or pastry cases (pie crusts). Try pork and diced apple; chicken and grapes; ham, peas and sweetcorn; or bacon, sliced mushrooms and green pepper.

Avocado and Prawn

METRIC/IMPERIAL	AMERICAN
100 g/4 oz peeled prawns	$\frac{1}{4}$ lb shelled shrimp
lemon juice	lemon juice
2 ripe avocados, stoned	2 ripe avocados, seeded
4 tablespoons mayonnaise	4 tablespoons mayonnaise
1 teaspoon paprika	1 teaspoon mild paprika
To garnish:	**To garnish:**
4 slices of lemon	4 slices of lemon
sprigs of parsley	sprigs of parsley

Toss the prawns (shrimp) in a little lemon juice and divide between the avocado halves.

Place a tablespoon of mayonnaise over the prawns in each avocado and sprinkle with paprika. Chill slightly before serving on individual plates, garnished with lemon and parsley.
Serves 4

Edam Dip

METRIC/IMPERIAL
1 Edam cheese
150 ml/¼ pint plain
    yogurt
4 tablespoons
    mayonnaise
about 450 ml/¾ pint
    milk
salt
freshly ground black
    pepper
To serve:
sticks of celery, carrot,
    cucumber,
    cauliflower florets
savoury biscuits

AMERICAN
1 Edam cheese
⅔ cup plain yogurt
4 tablespoons
    mayonnaise
about 2 cups milk
salt
freshly ground black
    pepper
To serve:
stalks of celery, carrot,
    cucumber,
    cauliflower florets
melba toast

Insert a sharp-pointed knife into the upper third of the Edam, and make zig-zag cuts to the centre of the cheese until the top of the cheese comes away in one piece. Lift off the top, scoop out the cheese in the centre and grate.

Mix the grated cheese with the yogurt and the mayonnaise. Add the chosen flavouring (see below) and stir in the milk gradually to make a soft consistency. Refill the Edam shell. Serve on a tray surrounded by the raw vegetables and savoury biscuits (melba toast).

Flavourings:

Curry and Fruit Add one 425 g/15 oz can crushed pineapple; 1 chopped eating apple and 2 tablespoons curry powder.

Spicy Mushroom Omit yogurt from the basic dip and add ½ pint/300 ml (1¼ cups) soured cream; 225 g/8 oz (1 cup) chopped mushrooms; 1 large finely chopped onion; 1 tablespoon chopped parsley and a dash of Tabasco sauce (hot pepper sauce).

Tangy Salmon Add one 198 g/7 oz can salmon, drained and flaked, and 1 tablespoon each of Worcestershire sauce, tomato ketchup and wine vinegar.

Serves 8 to 10

Summer Pork Round

METRIC/IMPERIAL
4 rashers of streaky
    bacon
175 g/6 oz fresh white
    breadcrumbs
450 g/1 lb pork
    sausagemeat
1 onion, chopped
½ green pepper, cored,
    seeded and finely
    chopped
1 tablespoon
    Worcestershire
    sauce
1 tablespoon tomato
    purée
2 teaspoons French
    mustard
1 teaspoon dried
    mixed herbs
1 egg, beaten
salt
freshly ground black
    pepper
rings of green pepper
    to garnish

AMERICAN
4 bacon slices
3 cups soft white
    bread crumbs
1 lb pork sausage-
    meat
1 onion, chopped
½ green pepper, cored,
    seeded, and finely
    chopped
1 tablespoon
    Worcestershire
    sauce
1 tablespoon tomato
    paste
2 teaspoons Dijon-
    style mustard
1 teaspoon dried
    mixed herbs
1 egg, beaten
salt
freshly ground black
    pepper
rings of green pepper
    to garnish

Line the base of a greased 15 cm/6 inch round cake tin (cake pan) with greaseproof (waxed) paper. Remove the rind from the bacon and arrange the slices over the bottom, trimming them to fit. Combine all the remaining ingredients in a large bowl and spoon the mixture into the tin (pan) levelling the mixture well with the back of a spoon. Cover with foil, and place in a preheated moderate oven (180°C/350°F, Gas Mark 4) and cook for 1¼ to 1½ hours. Allow to cool in the tin (pan) with a weight on the top.

Turn out (unmold) onto a serving dish and garnish with green pepper.

Serves 6

Danish Blue Cheese Mousse

METRIC/IMPERIAL	AMERICAN
1 tablespoon gelatine	1 tablespoon unflavored gelatin
2 tablespoons water	2 tablespoons water
300 ml/½ pint double cream, whipped	1¼ cups heavy cream, whipped
100 g/4 oz Danish Blue cheese, grated	1 cup crumbled blue cheese
100 g/4 oz Samsoe cheese, grated	1 cup grated Samsoe cheese
25 g/1 oz flaked almonds, toasted and chopped	¼ cup toasted and chopped almonds
2 egg whites	2 egg whites
pinch of dry mustard	pinch of dry mustard
freshly ground black pepper	freshly ground black pepper

Place the gelatine in a small bowl with the water and heat over a pan of hot water (double-boiler) until dissolved. Allow to cool. In a large bowl mix the cream, cheeses and almonds and stir in the gelatine.

In a bowl whisk the egg whites until stiff and fold carefully into the cheese mixture. Add the mustard and pepper to taste. Pour into a 600 ml/1 pint (2½ cup) ring mould or individual ramekin dishes. Chill until set.
Serves 8

Smoked Haddock and Egg Pâté

METRIC/IMPERIAL	AMERICAN
350 g/12 oz smoked haddock fillets	¾ lb smoked haddock fillets
150 ml/¼ pint milk	⅔ cup milk
150 g/5 oz butter, softened	½ cup + 2 tablespoons butter, softened
2 sprigs of parsley	2 sprigs of parsley
1 tablespoon lemon juice	1 tablespoon lemon juice
¼ teaspoon grated nutmeg	¼ teaspoon grated nutmeg
freshly ground black pepper	freshly ground black pepper
2 hard-boiled eggs, chopped	2 hard-cooked eggs, chopped
To garnish:	**To garnish:**
1 slice of lemon	1 slice of lemon
sprigs of parsley	sprigs of parsley

In a shallow pan, poach the haddock in the milk with 2 tablespoons of the butter and the parsley sprigs for about 15 minutes. Lift out the fish, remove the skin and bones and flake. Place in a small bowl and mix with the remaining ingredients. Transfer to a serving dish and garnish with lemon and parsley. Serve with potato crisps (chips).
Serves 6 to 8

Ham and Spinach Fingers

METRIC/IMPERIAL	AMERICAN
Shortcrust Pastry:	**Basic Pie Dough:**
175 g/6 oz plain flour	1½ cups all-purpose flour
75 g/3 oz butter	6 tablespoons butter
50 g/2 oz cheese, grated	½ cup grated cheese
3–4 tablespoons water	3–4 tablespoons water
Filling:	**Filling:**
4 slices cooked ham, chopped	4 slices cooked ham, chopped
1 × 225 g/8 oz packet frozen spinach, completely thawed	1 × ½ lb packet frozen spinach, completely thawed
150 ml/¼ pint milk	⅔ cup milk
1 egg, beaten	1 egg, beaten
100 g/4 oz cheese, grated	1 cup grated cheese
salt	salt
freshly ground black pepper	freshly ground black pepper

To make the pastry (dough), place the flour in a large bowl and rub (cut) in the butter until the mixture resembles fine breadcrumbs. Stir in the cheese, add the water and form into a soft ball. Roll out and use to line a 33 × 23 cm/13 × 9 inch Swiss roll tin (jelly roll pan). Mix all the ingredients for the filling in a large bowl and pour into the lined tin (pan). Place in a pre-heated moderately hot oven (190°C/375°F, Gas Mark 5) and cook for 30 to 40 minutes. Serve hot or cold, cut into fingers.
Serves 8 to 12

Meat Dishes

Select prime cuts of lamb, beef or pork and choose meat pieces that are roughly the same size and thickness so that they cook evenly. Use scissors to snip the edges of large steaks and chops to prevent them curling up during cooking, and use a marinade. A marinade enhances the flavour of the meat and it also has a tenderizing effect. Use leftover marinade to baste the meat while cooking; this prevents the meat from drying out.

Devilled Lamb Chops

METRIC/IMPERIAL	AMERICAN
4 lamb leg bone chops	4 leg lamb chops
salt	salt
freshly ground black pepper	freshly ground black pepper
4 teaspoons French mustard	4 teaspoons Dijon-style mustard
4 tablespoons demerara sugar	4 tablespoons firmly packed brown sugar

Trim the chops, sprinkle with salt and pepper and spread with half the mustard and sugar. Place over medium hot coals and cook gently for 7 to 10 minutes. Turn over and spread the remaining mustard and sugar over the chops. Cook for a further 7 to 10 minutes.
Serves 4
Note:
When grilling lamb chops and cutlets choose loin, chump, best end of neck cutlets (rib chops) and boneless slices (steaks) from the top of the leg. Allow 1 to 2 chops for each person.
Approximate cooking time for lamb:
Loin chops – 10 minutes each side
Chump chops (English lamb chops) – 12 minutes each side
Cutlets (Frenched rib chops) – 7 minutes each side
Leg chops – 10 minutes each side

Spicy Lamb Bake

METRIC/IMPERIAL	AMERICAN
6 lamb loin chops	6 loin lamb chops
50 g/2 oz butter, melted	$\frac{1}{4}$ cup melted butter
salt	salt
freshly ground black pepper	freshly ground black pepper
2 onions, sliced in rings	2 onions, sliced in rings
2 cloves garlic, crushed	2 cloves garlic, crushed
1 teaspoon ground ginger	1 teaspoon ground ginger
1 teaspoon ground allspice	1 teaspoon ground allspice
1 teaspoon dried rosemary	1 teaspoon dried rosemary
2 tablespoons honey	2 tablespoons honey
fresh sprigs of rosemary to garnish	fresh sprigs of rosemary to garnish

Brush the chops with butter on both sides and sprinkle with salt and pepper. Set aside. In a frying pan (skillet), sauté the onions and garlic in the remaining butter for 3 minutes. Add the ginger, allspice and rosemary, mix and cook for 1 minute. Add the honey and stir well.

Cut 6 square pieces of double aluminium foil and place a chop in the centre of each piece. Divide the onion mixture between them, placing some on each chop.

Seal the edges of the foil well to form individual parcels. Place on the barbecue grill over medium hot coals and cook for about 30 minutes. Serve, garnished with sprigs of rosemary.
Serves 6

Spicy Lamb Bake
(Photograph: Gale's Honey Bureau)

Gingered Pork Chops

METRIC/IMPERIAL	AMERICAN
4 pork loin chops	4 loin pork chops
Marinade:	**Marinade:**
2 tablespoons chopped stem ginger	2 tablespoons chopped preserved ginger
1 tablespoon soy sauce	1 tablespoon soy sauce
1 tablespoon tomato purée	1 tablespoon tomato paste
2 spring onions, chopped	2 scallions, chopped
6 tablespoons white wine	6 tablespoons white wine
salt	salt
freshly ground black pepper	freshly ground black pepper

Place the meat in a shallow dish. Combine the marinade ingredients in a small saucepan and heat gently for 5 minutes. Pour over the meat, cover and leave for approximately 2 to 3 hours or preferably overnight in the refrigerator.

Drain the chops and reserve marinade. Place on an oiled barbecue grill over medium hot coals. Cook for about 12 minutes on each side, brushing frequently with the marinade. Serve any remaining marinade as a sauce.

Serves 4

London Grill with Piquant Sauce

METRIC/IMPERIAL	AMERICAN
4 tablespoons Worcestershire sauce	4 tablespoons Worcestershire sauce
2 tablespoons oil	2 tablespoons oil
4 tablespoons water	4 tablespoons water
juice of ½ lemon	juice of ½ lemon
salt	salt
1 boned beef topside, about 1 kg/2 lb	1 beef top round, about 2 lb
Piquant Sauce:	**Piquant Sauce:**
75 g (3 oz) butter	6 tablespoons butter
2 teaspoons made English mustard	2 teaspoons prepared English mustard
2 tablespoons Worcestershire sauce	2 tablespoons Worcestershire sauce
6 gherkins, chopped	6 gherkins, chopped
2 tablespoons double cream	2 tablespoons heavy cream

Mix the Worcestershire sauce, oil, water, lemon juice and salt in a bowl. Place the meat in a large shallow dish and pour the mixture over the top.

Leave to marinate overnight, or for at least 6 hours, turning once.

Melt the butter in a saucepan, remove from the heat and stir in the remaining sauce ingredients. Allow to cool.

Remove the meat from the marinade and pierce lengthwise with a long skewer. Spread with a little sauce. Place the meat over hot coals and cook for about 10 minutes on each side for a rare-cooked steak, longer for a well-done steak. Spread with more sauce two or three times during cooking. To carve, place the meat on a serving board and cut at a slight angle, into thin slices.

Serves 4 to 6

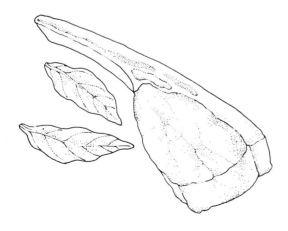

Gammon Steaks with Lemon Glaze

METRIC/IMPERIAL	AMERICAN
100 g/4 oz soft brown sugar	1 cup firmly packed light brown sugar
3 tablespoons made mustard	3 tablespoons prepared mustard
2 tablespoons lemon juice	2 tablespoons lemon juice
½ teaspoon grated lemon rind	½ teaspoon grated lemon rind
6 gammon steaks	6 ham steaks
To garnish:	**To garnish:**
6 thin slices of lemon	6 thin slices of lemon
sprigs of watercress	sprigs of watercress

Mix the sugar, mustard, lemon juice and rind in a small bowl. Snip the fat around the meat at regular intervals. Brush the lemon glaze over the steaks, and place on a well-oiled barbecue grill over medium hot coals. Cook for about 6 to 8 minutes on each side, basting continually with the remaining glaze. When the steaks are cooked through and the glaze is golden brown and sticky, garnish each steak with a slice of lemon and sprig of watercress. Serve immediately.
Serves 6

Honeyed Pork

METRIC/IMPERIAL	AMERICAN
4 lean pork chops	4 lean center cut pork chops
4 tablespoons clear honey	4 tablespoons honey
1 tablespoon oil	1 tablespoon oil
1–2 cloves garlic, crushed	1–2 cloves garlic, crushed
3 tablespoons medium sherry	3 tablespoons cream sherry
salt	salt
freshly ground black pepper	freshly ground black pepper
25 g/1 oz flaked almonds (optional)	¼ cup sliced almonds (optional)

Lay the chops in a shallow dish. Mix the remaining ingredients except the nuts together in a bowl and pour over the chops. Cover and leave in a cool place for about 5 to 6 hours turning occasionally. Remove the chops from the marinade and place on a well-oiled bar-becue grill over medium hot coals. Cook for about 10 to 12 minutes each side, basting frequently with marinade during cooking.

If wished, serve each chop with almonds sprinkled over the top.
Serves 4
Note:
Suitable pork cuts to barbecue are: loin chops, leg steaks and spareribs (country-style pork ribs).

Sweet and Sour Steaks

METRIC/IMPERIAL	AMERICAN
4 sirloin or rump steaks	4 top round steaks
Marinade:	**Marinade:**
2 tablespoons soy sauce	2 tablespoons soy sauce
4 tablespoons pineapple juice	4 tablespoons pineapple juice
1 tablespoon ground ginger	1 tablespoon ground ginger
2 tablespoons medium sherry	2 tablespoons cream sherry
½ teaspoon dry mustard	½ teaspoon dry mustard
1 clove garlic, crushed	1 clove garlic, crushed
25 g/1 oz butter, melted	2 tablespoons melted butter

Place the meat in a large shallow dish. In a bowl, mix together all the remaining ingredients except the butter and pour over the steaks. Cover and stand for at least 4 hours. Drain the meat and reserve the marinade. Place the meat on a well-oiled barbecue grill over medium hot coals and cook for 5 to 7 minutes each side, according to taste. Baste occasionally with the melted butter during cooking.

Heat the remaining marinade in a small saucepan and pour a little over each steak before serving.
Serves 4

Pork and Rice Parcels

METRIC/IMPERIAL	AMERICAN
4 lean pork loin chops	4 lean pork loin chops
salt	salt
freshly ground black pepper	freshly ground black pepper
1 tablespoon soy sauce	1 tablespoon soy sauce
175 g/6 oz cooked long-grain rice	1½ cups cooked long-grain rice
1 × 326 g/11½ oz can sweetcorn, drained	1 × 12 oz can whole kernel corn, drained
4 spring onions, chopped	4 scallions, chopped
4 tablespoons dry cider	4 tablespoons hard cider

Cut 4 large squares of double aluminium foil and put a chop in the centre of each piece. Sprinkle each with salt and pepper and soy sauce.

In a bowl, mix together the rice, sweetcorn and onions (scallions). Put one quarter of the mixture on top of each chop. Add a tablespoon of cider to each and seal the edges of the foil well to form 4 individual parcels. Place on the barbecue grill over medium hot coals and cook for about 35 minutes or until the meat is tender.
Serves 4

Note:
Aluminium cooking foil makes an airtight parcel, retaining all the moisture and delicate flavour of the food inside. Use double foil to give extra strength and fold each join twice to make it airtight.

Blue Cheese Gammon

METRIC/IMPERIAL	AMERICAN
75 g/3 oz butter, softened	6 tablespoons softened butter
75 g/3 oz Danish blue cheese, crumbled	½ cup crumbled blue cheese
salt	salt
freshly ground black pepper	freshly ground black pepper
4 gammon steaks	4 ham steaks
oil for brushing	oil for brushing
6 spring onions, chopped	6 scallions, chopped
grated rind and juice of 2 oranges	grated rind and juice of 2 oranges
4 thick slices of orange	4 thick slices of orange

Make the blue cheese butter in advance. Mix the butter, cheese and salt and pepper together and form into a sausage shape. Roll up in a piece of greaseproof (waxed) paper or foil, twisting each end of the paper to seal. Chill for 30 minutes to 1 hour in the freezer or ice compartment of the refrigerator until firm.

Snip the fat around the meat at regular intervals and brush with oil. Place on an oiled barbecue grill over medium hot coals and cook for about 6 minutes. Turn the steaks over, brush with oil and sprinkle with the onions (scallions), orange rind and juice. Continue cooking until the meat is tender.

Top each steak with a slice of orange and a slice of blue cheese butter.
Serves 4

Note:
The blue cheese butter can be frozen in foil. Store for up to 6 months. Allow to thaw slightly before slicing.

Blue Cheese Gammon
(Photograph: British Bacon Bureau)

Pork and Sage Bake

METRIC/IMPERIAL
4 lean pork chops
salt
freshly ground black
    pepper
2 onions, finely
    chopped
100 g/4 oz mature
    Cheddar cheese,
    grated
1 tablespoon chopped
    sage
2 tablespoons lemon
    juice
1 cooking apple,
    peeled, cored and
    sliced

AMERICAN
4 lean center cut pork
    chops
salt
freshly ground black
    pepper
2 onions, finely
    chopped
1 cup grated sharp
    Cheddar cheese
1 tablespoon chopped
    sage
2 tablespoons lemon
    juice
1 tart apple, peeled,
    cored and sliced

Cut 4 pieces of double aluminium foil, large enough to parcel each chop. Place one chop in the centre of each piece of foil and sprinkle with salt and pepper. In a bowl, mix the onions, cheese and sage and divide the mixture equally over the chops.

Pour the lemon juice into a shallow dish and toss the apple slices until evenly coated. Drain.

Place slices of apple over the cheese topping, and seal the edges of the foil well to form individual parcels. Place on the barbecue grill over medium hot coals and cook for about 30 to 35 minutes or until the meat is tender.
Serves 4
Note:
Cook pork until the juices run out clear. If the juices are slightly pink-tinged, continue cooking, as pork should never be undercooked.

Western Steak Barbecue

METRIC/IMPERIAL
2 rashers of bacon
2 tablespoons oil
1 onion, finely
    chopped
4 tablespoons lemon
    juice
1 tablespoon tomato
    ketchup
1 tablespoon
    Worcestershire
    sauce
1 tablespoon
    horseradish sauce
salt
freshly ground black
    pepper
4 rump steaks

AMERICAN
4 bacon slices
2 tablespoons oil
1 onion, finely
    chopped
4 tablespoons lemon
    juice
1 tablespoon ketchup
1 tablespoon
    Worcestershire
    sauce
1 tablespoon creamy
    horseradish sauce
salt
freshly ground black
    pepper
4 top round steaks

Remove the rind from the bacon and cut into small pieces. Heat the oil in a saucepan and sauté the onion and bacon until the onion is soft and lightly brown. Stir in the lemon juice, ketchup, Worcestershire and horseradish sauces and salt and pepper to taste. Mix well. Place the steaks in a shallow dish and pour over the marinade. Cover and leave for at least 1 hour, turning the steak at least once.

Drain the steaks, reserving the marinade, and place on a well-oiled barbecue grill over medium hot coals. Cook for about 5 to 7 minutes each side, according to taste. Baste two or three times with the marinade during cooking. Serve the steaks on a bed of rice.
Serves 4

Foil-Wrapped Veal

METRIC/IMPERIAL	AMERICAN
4 veal loin chops	4 veal loin chops
3 tomatoes, skinned and chopped	3 tomatoes, peeled and chopped
1 large onion, finely chopped	1 large onion, finely chopped
1 tablespoon finely chopped chives	1 tablespoon finely chopped chives
½ teaspoon each dried tarragon and dried marjoram	½ teaspoon each dried tarragon and dried marjoram
4 tablespoons oil	4 tablespoons oil
4 tablespoons medium sherry	4 tablespoons cream sherry

Cut 4 large squares of double aluminium foil and put a chop in the centre of each.

In a bowl, mix the tomatoes, onion, chives, tarragon and marjoram. Place a quarter of this mixture on each chop. In a small bowl, mix the oil and sherry and spoon 2 tablespoons of the mixture over each chop. Seal the edges of the foil well to form 4 individual parcels. Place on the barbecue grill over medium hot coals and cook for about 30 minutes or until the meat is tender. Turn once during cooking.
Serves 4

Pineapple and Gammon Parcels

METRIC/IMPERIAL	AMERICAN
4 gammon steaks	4 ham steaks
4 pineapple rings	4 pineapple rings
2 tablespoons demerara sugar	2 tablespoons firmly packed brown sugar
2 tablespoons Worcestershire sauce	2 tablespoons Worcestershire sauce
1 teaspoon dry mustard	1 teaspoon dry mustard

Place each steak on a square piece of double aluminium foil and top with a pineapple ring. In a small bowl, mix the sugar, Worcestershire sauce and mustard and spoon equally over the pineapple.

Seal the edges of the foil well to form 4 parcels. Place on the barbecue grill over medium hot coals and cook for about 15 minutes. Serve straight from the foil.
Serves 4

Garlic Steaks

METRIC/IMPERIAL	AMERICAN
6 rump steaks, cut 2.5 cm/1 inch thick	6 top round steaks, cut 1 inch thick
50 g/2 oz butter, melted	¼ cup melted butter
3 cloves garlic, crushed	3 cloves garlic, crushed
juice of 2 lemons	juice of 2 lemons
2 tablespoons Worcestershire sauce	2 tablespoons Worcestershire sauce
salt	salt
freshly ground black pepper	freshly ground black pepper

Beat the steaks until 0.5 cm/¼ inch thick. Mix the butter and garlic in a small bowl and brush evenly over the meat. Place the meat on a well-oiled barbecue grill over medium hot coals and cook for about 5 minutes on each side, according to taste. Baste during cooking with the garlic butter.

Add the lemon juice, Worcestershire sauce and salt and pepper to the remaining garlic butter, mix well and spread a little over each steak before serving.
Serves 6
Note:
Suitable cuts of beef are: fillet (tenderloin) steak, rump steak and sirloin steak (top round steaks).

Kebabs

A kebab party can be fun. Offer your guests a variety of meats, fish, vegetables and fruits, bearing in mind colour and flavour contrasts. Let your guests make their own meal-on-a-stick! As a general rule, only the tender boneless cuts of meat should be used, but sausages and bacon rolls can also be delicious.

Lamb Kebabs with Mint Dip

METRIC/IMPERIAL	AMERICAN
750 g/1½ lb boned fillet, leg end of lamb	1½ lb boned tenderloin leg end of lamb
300 ml/½ pint plain yogurt	1¼ cups plain yogurt
1 tablespoon olive oil	1 tablespoon olive oil
2 teaspoons concentrated mint sauce	2 teaspoons concentrated mint sauce
salt	salt
freshly ground black pepper	freshly ground black pepper
50 g/2 oz cream cheese, softened	¼ cup cream cheese, softened

Place the meat in a shallow dish. In a bowl, mix half the yogurt with the olive oil and 1 teaspoon of the mint sauce. Pour over the lamb, cover and marinate for about 1 hour. Drain and thread the meat onto 4 oiled kebab skewers and sprinkle with salt and pepper. Place over medium hot coals and cook for about 15 minutes, turning frequently until the meat is tender.

Meanwhile, in a bowl, mix the remaining yogurt and mint sauce with the cream cheese. Add pepper to taste. Serve with the kebabs.
Serves 4

Chicken Kebabs with Carrot Rice

METRIC/IMPERIAL	AMERICAN
200 g/7 oz long-grain rice	1 cup long-grain rice
600 ml/1 pint water	2½ cups water
salt	salt
1 tablespoon vinegar	1 tablespoon vinegar
1 teaspoon honey	1 teaspoon honey
1 tablespoon oil	1 tablespoon oil
freshly ground black pepper	freshly ground black pepper
ground ginger to taste	ground ginger to taste
225 g/8 oz carrots, cut in julienne strips	½ lb carrots, cut in julienne strips
450 g/1 lb chicken breast, cut in bite-sized pieces	1 lb chicken breast cut in bite-sized pieces
4 medium onions, cut into 8	4 medium onions, cut into 8
225 g/8 oz mushrooms	2 cups mushrooms
1 tablespoon paprika	1 tablespoon mild paprika
few drops Tabasco sauce	few drops hot pepper sauce

Put the rice, water and salt into a saucepan. Bring to the boil and stir once. Lower the heat to simmer, cover and cook for 15 minutes or until the rice is tender and the liquid absorbed. Remove from the heat and allow to cool. To make the marinade, mix the vinegar, honey, 1 teaspoon of oil, pepper and ginger in a large bowl. Add the rice and carrots. Leave to stand for 2 hours.

Thread the chicken, onions and mushrooms onto oiled skewers. In a bowl, mix the remaining oil, paprika, salt and Tabasco (hot pepper) sauce and brush over the kebabs. Place over medium hot coals and cook for about 15 minutes, turning and basting occasionally.
Serves 4

*Chicken Kebabs with Carrot Rice
(Photograph: US Rice Council)*

Bacon Kebabs with Seville Sauce

METRIC/IMPERIAL	AMERICAN
1 tablespoon oil	1 tablespoon oil
2 tablespoons Worcestershire sauce	2 tablespoons Worcestershire sauce
juice and rind of 1 large orange	juice and rind of 1 large orange
salt	salt
freshly ground black pepper	freshly ground black pepper
450 g/1 lb vacuum-packed shoulder bacon joint cut into 2.5 cm/1 inch cubes	1 lb vacuum-packed smoked picnic shoulder bacon cut into 1 inch cubes
4 thin skinless pork sausages, halved	4 thin skinless pork sausage links, halved
8 small onions, parboiled	8 pearl onions, parboiled
12 button mushrooms	12 small mushrooms
Sauce:	**Sauce:**
2 teaspoons cornflour	2 teaspoons cornstarch
150 ml/¼ pint water	⅔ cup water
3 tablespoons chunky marmalade	3 tablespoons chunky marmalade

To make the marinade, mix the oil, Worcestershire sauce, orange rind and juice, salt and pepper in a shallow dish.

Add the bacon cubes to the marinade and leave for at least 2 hours, turning occasionally. Drain the bacon, reserving the marinade, and thread onto 4 oiled skewers, alternating with the sausages, onions and mushrooms. Brush with the marinade. Place on a well-oiled barbecue grill over medium hot coals and cook for 12 to 15 minutes, turning frequently.

For the sauce, place the remaining marinade in a saucepan. In a cup, mix the cornflour (cornstarch) with a little of the water, stir into the marinade and add the rest of the water and the marmalade.

Bring to the boil, stirring, reduce heat and simmer gently for 2 minutes. Serve the kebabs with the sauce handed separately.
Serves 4

Sicilian Kebabs

METRIC/IMPERIAL	AMERICAN
2 whole chicken breasts, halved	2 whole chicken breasts, halved
12 rashers of bacon	12 bacon slices
4 continental or grilling sausages, thickly sliced	4 continental or grilling sausage links, thickly sliced
6 chicken livers, halved	6 chicken livers, halved
18 large mushroom caps	18 large mushroom caps
fresh bay leaves	fresh bay leaves
75 g/3 oz butter, melted	6 tablespoons melted butter
pinch mixed herbs	pinch mixed herbs
2 teaspoons paprika	2 teaspoons mild paprika

If using bamboo skewers, as in the illustration, stand them in water for 10 minutes before use. Cut each piece of chicken in 6 chunks. Remove the rind from the bacon and cut each slice in 4. Thread 6 skewers, alternating chicken chunks, sausages, livers, bacon, mushrooms and bay leaves.

Brush with melted butter and sprinkle with herbs. Place over medium hot coals and cook for about 10 minutes, turning once or twice. Brush several times with the butter and sprinkle with paprika. Serve immediately.
Serves 6

Kidney Kebabs with Barbecue Sauce

METRIC/IMPERIAL	AMERICAN
6 rashers of streaky bacon	6 bacon slices
8 small onions, parboiled	8 pearl onions, parboiled
4 lambs' kidneys, halved and cored	4 lamb kidneys, halved and cored
4 skinless pork sausages, halved	4 skinless pork sausage links, halved
Baste:	**Baste:**
1 teaspoon tomato purée	1 teaspoon tomato paste
1 teaspoon Worcestershire sauce	1 teaspoon Worcestershire sauce
1 tablespoon oil	1 tablespoon oil
Sauce:	**Sauce:**
15 g/½ oz butter	1 tablespoon butter
1 onion, chopped	1 onion, chopped
150 ml/¼ pint tomato ketchup	⅔ cup ketchup
6 tablespoons Worcestershire sauce	6 tablespoons Worcestershire sauce
2 tablespoons clear honey	2 tablespoons honey
2 tablespoons lemon juice	2 tablespoons lemon juice
salt	salt
freshly ground black pepper	freshly ground black pepper

Remove the rind from the bacon and stretch the rashers (slices) on a board with the back of a round-bladed knife. Cut each in half. Roll up pieces of bacon and thread onto 4 oiled skewers alternating with onions, pieces of kidney and sausage.

For the baste, mix the ingredients in a small bowl and brush over the kebabs.

Place the kebabs over medium hot coals and cook for 4 to 5 minutes on each side, brushing with the baste during cooking.

For the sauce, melt the butter in a saucepan and sauté the onion gently for 5 minutes. Add the remaining ingredients, bring to the boil, reduce heat and simmer for 5 minutes. Serve with the kebabs.
Serves 4

Spiced Vegetable Kebabs

METRIC/IMPERIAL	AMERICAN
Baste:	**Baste:**
4 tablespoons tomato ketchup	4 tablespoons ketchup
4 tablespoons Worcestershire sauce	4 tablespoons Worcestershire sauce
1 tablespoon wine vinegar	1 tablespoon wine vinegar
1 tablespoon demerara sugar	1 tablespoon brown sugar
4 tablespoons oil	4 tablespoons oil
1 teaspoon made English mustard	1 teaspoon prepared English mustard
salt	salt
freshly ground black pepper	freshly ground black pepper
Kebabs:	**Kebabs:**
tomatoes, quartered	tomatoes, quartered
button mushrooms	small mushrooms
small onions, parboiled	pearl onions, parboiled
green and red pepper, cored, seeded and cut in chunks	green and red pepper, cored, seeded and cut in chunks
courgettes, cut in chunks	zucchini, cut in chunks

For the baste, place all the ingredients in a bowl and mix well. Make up the vegetable kebabs by threading selected vegetables alternately onto oiled skewers. Brush vegetables generously with the baste. Place over medium hot coals and cook for about 10 to 12 minutes, turning, until vegetables are cooked through and have begun to soften. Brush with the baste 2 or 3 times during cooking. To serve, spoon any extra baste over the kebabs.
Serves 6

Pasanda Tikka

METRIC/IMPERIAL	AMERICAN
350 g/12 oz lean pork, cut in 2.5 cm/1 inch cubes	3/4 lb lean pork, cut in 1 inch cubes
3–4 tablespoons plain yogurt	3–4 tablespoons plain yoghurt
1/2 teaspoon salt	1/2 teaspoon salt
2 teaspoons mild or hot curry paste	2 teaspoons mild or hot curry paste
75 g/3 oz butter, melted	6 tablespoons melted butter
To garnish:	**To garnish:**
2 onions, cut in rings	2 onions, cut in rings
1 lemon, sliced	1 lemon, sliced

Thoroughly prick the meat and place in a large shallow dish. In a bowl, mix the yogurt, salt and curry paste and pour over the meat. Cover and marinate for 6 hours. Drain and arrange the meat on 6 small, oiled skewers. Place on the barbecue over medium hot coals and cook for about 15 to 20 minutes. Turn and brush occasionally with melted butter. Serve garnished with onion and lemon.
Serves 3 to 6

Shish Kebab

METRIC/IMPERIAL	AMERICAN
350 g/12 oz minced beef or lamb	3/4 lb ground beef or lamb
1 onion, chopped	1 onion, chopped
2 teaspoons lemon juice	2 teaspoons lemon juice
2 teaspoons medium or hot curry powder	2 teaspoons medium or hot curry powder
1 tablespoon plain yogurt	1 tablespoon plain yogurt
1 egg, beaten	1 egg, beaten
2 tablespoons plain flour	2 tablespoons all-purpose flour
2 tablespoons chopped coriander	2 tablespoons chopped coriander
1/2 teaspoon salt	1/2 teaspoon salt
oil for brushing	oil for brushing

In a large bowl, mix all the ingredients except the oil until smooth. Divide into 6 and form into sausage shapes. Thread on to 2 oiled skewers. Refrigerate for 2 hours. Brush the meat with oil and cook over medium hot coals for 15 to 20 minutes, turning occasionally.
Serves 3 to 6

Tomato Beef Kebabs

METRIC/IMPERIAL	AMERICAN
Marinade:	**Marinade:**
1/2 × 326 g/11 1/2 oz can tomato juice	1/2 × 11 1/2 oz can tomato juice
generous pinch of garlic salt	generous pinch of garlic salt
pinch of mixed herbs	pinch of mixed herbs
salt	salt
freshly ground black pepper	freshly ground black pepper
1 tablespoon soy sauce	1 tablespoon soy sauce
Kebabs:	**Kebabs:**
450 g/1 lb rump steak, cut in 2.5 cm/1 inch cubes	1 lb top round steak, cut in 1 inch cubes
8 small onions, parboiled	8 pearl onions, parboiled
4 small tomatoes, halved	4 cherry tomatoes, halved
8 button mushrooms	8 small mushrooms
1 green and 1 red pepper, each cored, seeded and cut in 8	1 green and 1 red pepper, each cored, seeded and cut in 8

Mix all the marinade ingredients in a bowl. Place the meat in a shallow dish, pour the marinade over and marinate for at least 1 hour, turning several times. Drain the meat and reserve the marinade. Arrange the meat, onions, tomatoes, mushrooms and peppers alternately on 4 oiled skewers.

Place on the barbecue over medium hot coals and cook for about 15 to 20 minutes, turning occasionally and basting with the remaining marinade.
Serves 4
Variation:
Try marinating 450 g/1 lb cubed steak in a mixture of 2 tablespoons peanut butter and 3 tablespoons Worcestershire sauce. Leave, covered, for about 2 hours. Thread the meat onto skewers and barbecue in the normal way.

Tandoori Chicken (page 38), Shish Kebabs, Pasanda Tikka, Prawns Poona (page 46) and Naan Bread (page 53)
(Photograph: Sharwood's Indian Range)

Mackerel Kebabs

METRIC/IMPERIAL
2 × 450 g/1 lb
    mackerel, cleaned,
    boned and cut in
    2.5 cm/1 inch pieces
6 button onions,
    halved
8–12 button
    mushrooms
1 green pepper, cored,
    seeded and cut in
    strips
Marinade:
4 tablespoons dry
    cider
4 tablespoons olive oil
½ teaspoon salt
freshly ground black
    pepper
2 teaspoons oregano
To garnish:
lemon wedges

AMERICAN
2 × 1 lb mackerel,
    cleaned, boned and
    cut in 1 inch pieces
6 pearl onions, halved
8–12 button
    mushrooms
1 green pepper, cored,
    seeded and cut in
    strips
Marinade:
4 tablespoons hard
    cider
4 tablespoons olive oil
½ teaspoon salt
freshly ground black
    pepper
2 teaspoons oregano
To garnish:
lemon wedges

Thread the mackerel onto oiled skewers, alternating with the vegetables. Place the kebabs in a shallow dish. In a bowl, combine the ingredients for the marinade and pour over the kebabs. Marinate for about 1 hour. Drain kebabs and reserve marinade.

Place the kebabs on a barbecue over medium hot coals and cook for 8 to 10 minutes, basting with the marinade and turning once. Serve garnished with lemon wedges.
Serves 4

Fish Kebabs with Herb Butter

METRIC/IMPERIAL
Herb Butter:
75 g/3 oz butter
1 tablespoon each
    finely chopped
    fresh dill, tarragon
    and chives
1 tablespoon lemon
    juice
salt
freshly ground black
    pepper
Kebabs:
8 rashers of streaky
    bacon
100 g/4 oz button
    mushrooms
450 g/1 lb cod steaks,
    cut in 5 cm/2 inch
    cubes
4 tomatoes, quartered
2 green peppers,
    cored, seeded and
    cut in chunks
225 g/8 oz plaice fillet,
    skinned and cut in
    squares
salt
freshly ground black
    pepper

AMERICAN
Herb Butter:
6 tablespoons butter
1 tablespoon each
    finely chopped
    fresh dill, tarragon
    and chives
1 tablespoon lemon
    juice
salt
freshly ground black
    pepper
Kebabs:
8 bacon slices
1 cup small
    mushrooms
1 lb cod steaks, cut in
    2 inch cubes
4 tomatoes, quartered
2 green peppers,
    cored, seeded and
    cut in chunks
8 oz flounder fillet,
    skinned and cut in
    squares
salt
freshly ground black
    pepper

Melt the butter in a small saucepan, add the herbs, lemon juice and salt and pepper and mix well. Remove the rind from the bacon and roll up each slice. Make up the kebabs by threading the prepared ingredients onto 3 to 4 oiled skewers. Brush the kebabs with the herb butter and place on the barbecue over medium hot coals for about 8 to 10 minutes, turning and basting 2 or 3 times during cooking. Serve the kebabs with the remaining butter poured over the top.
Serves 3 to 4

Saucy Mixed Kebabs

METRIC/IMPERIAL	AMERICAN
8 rashers of bacon	8 bacon slices
1 × 340 g/12 oz can pineapple chunks	1 × ¾ lb can pineapple chunks
225 g/8 oz cooked chicken, in large chunks	½ lb cooked chicken, in large chunks
2 tomatoes, quartered	2 tomatoes, quartered
225 g/8 oz Edam cheese, cut in triangles	½ lb Edam cheese, cut in triangles
¼ cucumber, cut in chunks	¼ cucumber, cut in chunks
Sauce:	**Sauce:**
1 tablespoon cornflour	1 tablespoon cornstarch
300 ml/½ pint dry cider	1¼ cups hard cider
1 tablespoon soft brown sugar	1 tablespoon firmly packed light brown sugar
1 tablespoon wine vinegar	1 tablespoon wine vinegar
½ teaspoon soy sauce	½ teaspoon soy sauce
salt	salt
freshly ground black pepper	freshly ground black pepper

Remove the rind from the bacon. Drain the pineapple chunks. Reserve 8 whole chunks for kebabs. Chop the remaining chunks finely and set aside for the sauce.

Wrap a slice of bacon around each pineapple chunk. Secure with cocktail sticks (toothpicks), place on an oiled barbecue grill over medium hot coals and cook for 4 to 5 minutes, turning occasionally until crisp all over. Remove the cocktail sticks (toothpicks). Thread the bacon rolls onto 8 oiled skewers, alternating with the remaining kebab ingredients. Place on the barbecue over medium hot coals and cook until the cheese begins to soften. Do not allow the cheese to melt.

In a cup, mix the cornflour (cornstarch) with 2 tablespoons of cider. Heat the remaining cider in a saucepan. Remove from the heat and add the cornflour (cornstarch) mixture. Return the pan to the heat and bring to the boil, stirring continuously.

Add the reserved chopped pineapple, sugar, vinegar, soy sauce and salt and pepper. Pour a little sauce over the kebabs and serve immediately. Pour the remaining sauce into a bowl and hand round separately.
Serves 4

Bacon and Corn Kebabs

METRIC/IMPERIAL	AMERICAN
750 g/1½ lb bacon collar joint, cut in 2 thick slices	1½ lb smoked shoulder butt bacon, cut in 2 thick slices
Marinade:	**Marinade:**
2 tablespoons Worcestershire sauce	2 tablespoons Worcestershire sauce
2 teaspoons made mustard	2 teaspoons prepared mustard
juice of 1 lemon	juice of 1 lemon
1 tablespoon tomato purée	1 tablespoon tomato paste
salt	salt
freshly ground black pepper	freshly ground black pepper
3 tablespoons oil	3 tablespoons oil
Kebabs:	**Kebabs:**
1 green pepper, cored, seeded and cut in chunks	1 green pepper, cored, seeded and cut in chunks
1 onion, cut in chunks	1 onion, cut in chunks
1 corn cob, parboiled, cut in 2.5 cm/1 inch pieces	1 corn cob, parboiled, cut in 1 inch pieces

Soak the bacon for 4 hours in cold water. Remove and cut in neat cubes. Place in a large saucepan, cover with water and simmer for 20 minutes, then drain. Mix all the marinade ingredients together in a large bowl and stir in the bacon cubes while they are still warm. Allow to marinate for about 1 hour. Drain the bacon cubes, reserving the marinade, and thread onto 2 large or 4 small, oiled skewers, alternating with chunks of pepper, onion and corn. Brush the kebabs with some of the remaining marinade. Place on the barbecue over medium hot coals and cook for about 6 minutes.

Turn the kebabs, brush with more marinade and cook for a further 6 minutes. Serve hot with salad and jacket potatoes.
Serves 4

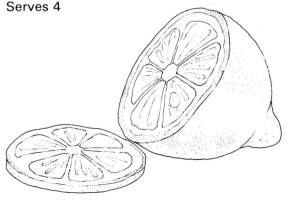

Barbecues on a Budget

Homemade burgers, sausages and some chicken joints are an economical alternative to steaks and chops, but take care not to overcook them or they will shrink and dry out.

Tomato Hamburgers

METRIC/IMPERIAL	AMERICAN
600 g/1¼ lb minced beef	1¼ lb ground beef
50 g/2 oz fresh breadcrumbs	1 cup fresh breadcrumbs
150 ml/¼ pint tomato purée	⅔ cup tomato paste
1 large onion, chopped	1 large onion, chopped
1 tablespoon chopped parsley	1 tablespoon chopped parsley
1 teaspoon Tabasco sauce	1 teaspoon hot pepper sauce
salt	salt
freshly ground black pepper	freshly ground black pepper

Mix all the ingredients in a bowl. Form into 10 cakes using a 5 cm (2 inch) scone cutter. Chill well, then cook on an oiled barbecue grid for about 5 minutes on each side.
Serves 5

Beachburgers

METRIC/IMPERIAL	AMERICAN
450 g/1 lb minced beef	1 lb ground beef
1 green pepper, cored, seeded and chopped	1 green pepper, cored, seeded and chopped
1 clove garlic, minced	1 clove garlic, minced
2 spring onions, finely chopped	2 scallions, finely chopped
2 tablespoons chopped parsley	2 tablespoons chopped parsley
large pinch of paprika	large pinch of paprika
salt	salt
freshly ground black pepper	freshly ground black pepper

Mix all the ingredients in a bowl. Form into 6 cakes using a 5 cm (2 inch) scone cutter. Chill well before cooking on an oiled barbecue grid for about 5 minutes on each side.
Serves 3 to 6

Irish Hamburgers

METRIC/IMPERIAL	AMERICAN
450 g/1 lb lean minced beef	1 lb ground beef
2 medium potatoes, peeled and grated	2 medium potatoes, peeled and grated
1 medium onion, peeled and finely chopped	1 medium onion, peeled and finely chopped
2 tablespoons chopped fresh parsley	2 tablespoons chopped fresh parsley
few drops of Worcestershire sauce	few drops of Worcestershire sauce
salt	salt
freshly ground black pepper	freshly ground black pepper

Put all the ingredients with salt and pepper to taste in a bowl and mix well together. Form into 8 cakes using a 5 cm (2 inch) scone cutter. Chill well before cooking on an oiled barbecue grid for about 5 minutes on each side. Serve topped with sliced tomato.
Serves 4

Beachburgers, Irish Hamburgers and Tomato Hamburgers

St Louis Rice Burgers

METRIC/IMPERIAL
Burgers:
450 g/1 lb lean minced
  beef
½ teaspoon dried
  mixed herbs
salt
freshly ground black
  pepper
1 small onion, finely
  chopped
1 clove garlic, crushed
175 g/6 oz cooked
  long-grain rice
1 egg, beaten
4 tablespoons white
  wine
1 tablespoon chopped
  parsley
To serve:
4 soft bread rolls,
  buttered
onion rings
selection of sauces or
  relishes

AMERICAN
Burgers:
1 lb ground beef
½ teaspoon dried
  mixed herbs
salt
freshly ground black
  pepper
1 small onion, finely
  chopped
1 clove garlic, crushed
1½ cups cooked long-
  grain rice
1 egg, beaten
4 tablespoons white
  wine
1 tablespoon chopped
  parsley
To serve:
4 burger buns,
  buttered
onion rings
selection of sauces or
  relishes

Place the meat in a large bowl and break up into small pieces. Add the remaining burger ingredients and mix well. Cover and leave to stand for at least 30 minutes.

Form into 4 thick patties, soft but not runny. Place the burgers on an oiled barbecue grill over medium hot coals and cook for about 7 minutes each side.

Serve each burger topped with onion rings in a buttered bread roll (bun), with sauces or relishes handed separately.

Serves 4

Hawaiian Lamb Burgers

METRIC/IMPERIAL
2 tablespoons oil
1 onion, finely
  chopped
1 clove garlic, crushed
450 g/1 lb lean minced
  lamb
1 stick celery, finely
  chopped
1 tablespoon tomato
  ketchup
1 teaspoon mixed
  herbs
50 g/2 oz fresh white
  breadcrumbs
salt
freshly ground black
  pepper
6 rashers of bacon
melted butter for
  brushing
6 canned pineapple
  rings

AMERICAN
2 tablespoons oil
1 onion, finely
  chopped
1 clove garlic, crushed
1 lb lean ground lamb
1 stalk celery, finely
  chopped
1 tablespoon ketchup
1 teaspoon mixed
  herbs
1 cup soft white bread
  crumbs
salt
freshly ground black
  pepper
6 bacon slices
melted butter for
  brushing
6 canned pineapple
  rings

Heat the oil in a frying pan (skillet) and sauté the onion and garlic until soft. Transfer to a large bowl and mix in the meat, celery, ketchup, herbs and breadcrumbs. Sprinkle with salt and pepper, mix well and shape into 6 patties. Remove the rind from the bacon and wrap a slice around each burger, securing it with a cocktail stick (toothpick). Brush each burger with a little melted butter and place on the oiled barbecue grill over medium hot coals. Cook for about 7 minutes each side. Brush the pineapple rings with melted butter and place on the oiled grill over medium hot coals until golden brown on both sides.

Top each burger with a slice of pineapple and serve immediately.

Serves 6

Mushroom Steaklets with Creamy Sauce

METRIC/IMPERIAL	AMERICAN
25 g/1 oz butter	2 tablespoons butter
2 tablespoons oil	2 tablespoons oil
2 onions, finely chopped	2 onions, finely chopped
225 g/8 oz mushrooms, finely chopped	2 cups finely chopped mushrooms
$\frac{1}{2}$ teaspoon dried sage	$\frac{1}{2}$ teaspoon dried sage
1 clove garlic, crushed	1 clove garlic, crushed
750 g/1$\frac{1}{2}$ lb minced beef	1$\frac{1}{2}$ lb ground beef
salt	salt
freshly ground black pepper	freshly ground black pepper
Creamy Sauce:	**Creamy Sauce:**
1 × 298 g/10$\frac{1}{2}$ oz can condensed mushroom soup	1 × 10$\frac{1}{2}$ oz can condensed mushroom soup
3 tablespoons soured cream	3 tablespoons sour cream
pinch mixed herbs	pinch mixed herbs

Heat the butter and oil in a saucepan and gently sauté the onions and mushrooms for 3 to 4 minutes. Mix in the sage and garlic and cook for a further minute. Allow the mixture to cool then mix with the meat, salt and pepper. Divide the mixture into 8 round shapes. Flatten and place on the oiled barbecue grill over medium hot coals. Cook for 5 to 6 minutes on each side.

Meanwhile make the sauce by mixing all the ingredients together in a small saucepan. Heat through gently, stirring once or twice. Pour a little sauce over each steaklet to serve and hand remaining sauce separately.
Serves 4 to 8

Cheese-Filled Sausages

METRIC/IMPERIAL	AMERICAN
8 thick pork sausages	8 thick pork sausage links
100 g/4 oz Cheddar cheese, grated	1 cup grated Cheddar cheese
8 rashers of bacon	8 bacon slices
2–3 tablespoons French mustard	2–3 tablespoons Dijon-style mustard

Place the sausages on the oiled barbecue grill over medium hot coals and cook for about 15 minutes. Slit the sausages lengthwise, almost cutting through. Place a little grated cheese in each sausage and press together again. Remove the rind from the bacon and spread each slice with a little mustard. Wrap a slice of bacon around each sausage, securing the ends with cocktail sticks (toothpicks).

Place on the barbecue again and, turning frequently, cook for about 5 minutes until the bacon is crisp and the fat is golden brown. Remove cocktail sticks (toothpicks) and serve.
Serves 4
Note:
To ensure that sausages keep their shape and do not split, place the raw sausages in a saucepan and cover with cold water. Bring to the boil, reduce heat and simmer for 1 to 2 minutes, then drain immediately. Barbecue in the usual way.

Hot Chilli Burgers

METRIC/IMPERIAL	AMERICAN
450 g/1 lb lean minced beef	1 lb lean ground beef
225 g/8 oz pork sausage meat	$\frac{1}{2}$ lb pork sausage meat
1 onion, grated	1 onion, minced
1 clove garlic, crushed	1 clove garlic, crushed
1 × 213 g/7$\frac{1}{2}$ oz can kidney beans, drained and chopped	1 × 8 oz can kidney beans, drained and chopped
2 teaspoons chilli powder	2 teaspoons chili powder
salt	salt
freshly ground black pepper	freshly ground black pepper
oil for brushing	oil for brushing
To serve:	**To serve:**
6–8 soft bread rolls	6–8 burger buns
2 tomatoes, sliced	2 tomatoes, sliced

Mix all the burger ingredients in a large bowl until smooth. Form the mixture into 6 or 8 neat rounds. Brush the burgers with oil and place on the barbecue grill over medium hot coals and cook for about 7 minutes on each side. Place the bread rolls (buns) at the side of the barbecue for 2 to 3 minutes to warm through. Serve each burger inside a bun, topped with tomato slices.
Serves 6 or 8

Barbecued Spareribs

METRIC/IMPERIAL	AMERICAN
1.5 kg/3 lb pork spareribs, in two pieces	3 lb pork spareribs, in two pieces
120 ml/4 fl oz soy sauce	$\frac{1}{2}$ cup soy sauce
2 cloves garlic, crushed	2 cloves garlic, crushed
2 tablespoons honey	2 tablespoons honey
2 tablespoons dry sherry	2 tablespoons dry sherry

Wipe the ribs with damp absorbent paper towels and place on a rack in a shallow roasting pan. Bake in a preheated moderate oven (180°C/350°F, Gas Mark 4) for 45 minutes, when excess fat will have cooked away. Pour the fat away and place the ribs in the pan. Mix the remaining ingredients, pour over the ribs and allow to marinate for 1 hour or so, or refrigerate overnight. Turn the ribs several times.

When ready to barbecue, place the ribs on the grill over coals until brown and crisp on both sides, basting with the marinade.
Serves 6

Herby Sausage Patties

METRIC/IMPERIAL	AMERICAN
450 g/1 lb pork sausagemeat	1 lb pork sausage-meat
2 teaspoons mixed herbs	2 teaspoons mixed herbs
1 clove garlic, crushed	1 clove garlic, crushed
2 tablespoons chopped parsley	2 tablespoons chopped parsley
salt	salt
freshly ground black pepper	freshly ground black pepper
1 × 446 g/15$\frac{1}{2}$ oz can baked beans	1 × 16 oz can baked beans

Mix all the ingredients, except the beans, in a large bowl. Divide the mixture into 6 and shape into patties. Place on an oiled barbecue grill over medium hot coals and cook for about 7 minutes each side. Meanwhile, heat the beans in a saucepan and serve poured over the cooked patties.
Serves 6

Sausages with Apricot Glaze

METRIC/IMPERIAL	AMERICAN
1 kg/2 lb thick sausages	2 lb thick sausage links
1 tablespoon oil	1 tablespoon oil
1 tablespoon vinegar	1 tablespoon vinegar
250 ml/8 fl oz canned apricots, puréed	1 cup canned apricots, puréed
4 tablespoons tomato ketchup	$\frac{1}{4}$ cup ketchup
1 tablespoon brown sugar	1 tablespoon brown sugar
1 tablespoon grated onion	1 tablespoon grated onion
$\frac{1}{2}$ teaspoon Worcestershire sauce	$\frac{1}{2}$ teaspoon Worcestershire sauce
$\frac{1}{4}$ teaspoon salt	$\frac{1}{4}$ teaspoon salt
$\frac{1}{2}$ teaspoon dried oregano	$\frac{1}{2}$ teaspoon dried oregano
dash of Tabasco or chilli sauce	dash of hot pepper or chili sauce

Prick the sausages in several places, place in a frying pan (skillet) with water to cover and simmer for 5 minutes, then drain.

Place the remaining ingredients in a saucepan, adding a little of the canned apricot syrup if necessary to give a thick sauce consistency. Simmer for 5 minutes, stirring now and again. Pour over the sausages and allow to stand for 30 minutes. Thread the sausages onto long skewers or simply place on grill bars and barbecue until crisp and brown on all sides, brushing frequently with the glaze. Spoon remaining glaze over the sausages to serve.
Serves 6 to 8

Barbecued Spareribs

Beefy Barbecue Sausages

METRIC/IMPERIAL	AMERICAN
8 thick beef sausages	8 thick beef sausage links
oil for brushing	oil for brushing
Barbecue Dip:	**Barbecue Dip:**
25 g/1 oz butter	2 tablespoons butter
1 small onion, chopped	1 small onion, chopped
2 rashers of streaky bacon, chopped	2 bacon slices, chopped
1 tablespoon tomato purée	1 tablespoon tomato paste
2 beef stock cubes, crumbled	4 beef bouillon cubes, crumbled
300 ml/½ pint dry cider	1¼ cups hard cider
25 g/1 oz demerara sugar	2 tablespoons, firmly packed, brown sugar
1 teaspoon Worcestershire sauce	1 teaspoon Worcestershire sauce

Melt the butter in a saucepan and sauté the onion and bacon gently until the onion is soft. Add the remaining dip ingredients and bring to the boil. Reduce heat and simmer for 15 minutes, stirring occasionally. Purée the sauce in a blender or food processor.

Brush the sausages with oil and place on the barbecue grill over medium hot coals. Cook for about 15 minutes, turning frequently. Serve the sausages hot or cold with the prepared dip.
Serves 4 to 8

Chicken Liver Roll-ups

METRIC/IMPERIAL	AMERICAN
225 g/8 oz prunes, soaked	8 oz prunes, soaked
450 g/1 lb chicken livers, trimmed	1 lb chicken livers, trimmed
225 g/8 oz rashers of bacon	½ lb bacon slices
Dressing:	**Dressing:**
1 tablespoon wine vinegar	1 tablespoon wine vinegar
salt and pepper	salt and pepper
3 tablespoons vegetable oil	3 tablespoons vegetable oil

Drain the prunes and place in a small bowl. Mix the vinegar with salt and pepper and beat in the oil with a fork or whisk. Pour the dressing over the prunes and set aside.

Cut the livers in halves if large. Remove the rind from the bacon and cut into pieces 8 to 10 cm/3 to 4 inches long.

Wrap a chicken liver and a prune in each piece of bacon and secure with a wooden cocktail stick (toothpick). Cook over hot coals for 3 to 4 minutes on each side. Brush with dressing once or twice each side.
Makes about 20

Swiss Cheeseburgers

METRIC/IMPERIAL	AMERICAN
450 g/1 lb lean minced beef	1 lb lean ground beef
25 g/1 oz fresh white breadcrumbs	½ cup soft white bread crumbs
1 tablespoon tomato purée	1 tablespoon tomato paste
100 g/4 oz Gruyère cheese, grated	1 cup grated Gruyère cheese
4 spring onions, finely chopped	4 scallions, finely chopped
2 tablespoons Worcestershire sauce	2 tablespoons Worcestershire sauce
1 egg, beaten	1 egg, beaten
salt	salt and freshly ground black pepper
freshly ground black pepper	
To serve:	**To serve:**
4 soft bread rolls, buttered	4 burger buns, buttered
shredded lettuce leaves	shredded lettuce leaves
2 tomatoes, sliced	2 tomatoes, sliced
small piece of cucumber, sliced	small piece of cucumber, sliced

Place all the burger ingredients in a large bowl and mix well. Form the mixture into 4 burgers, each 1 cm (½ inch) thick. Chill for 30 minutes. Place the burgers on an oiled barbecue grill over medium hot coals and cook for about 12 to 15 minutes, turning once.

Serve each inside a roll (bun) with lettuce, tomato and cucumber.
Serves 4

Porkburgers

METRIC/IMPERIAL	AMERICAN
450 g/1 lb pork sausagemeat or minced pork	1 lb pork sausagemeat or ground pork
2 bacon rashers, rinds removed, minced or finely chopped	2 bacon slices, rinds removed, ground or finely chopped
2 teaspoons Worcestershire sauce	2 teaspoons Worcestershire sauce
1 small onion, peeled and grated	1 small onion, peeled and grated
2 tablespoons fresh white breadcrumbs	2 tablespoons fresh white bread crumbs
salt	salt
freshly ground black pepper	freshly ground black pepper
2 teaspoons oil	2 teaspoons oil

Mix the sausagemeat or minced pork with the bacon, Worcestershire sauce, onion, breadcrumbs, and salt and pepper to taste. Shape into 6 cakes using a 6.5 cm (2½ inch) pastry cutter. Chill until firm. Brush with oil and cook over a hot barbecue, turning occasionally.

Serve topped with sliced tomatoes and placed in heated rolls or burger buns.
Serves 6

Saucy Barbecued Spareribs

METRIC/IMPERIAL	AMERICAN
6 pork sparerib chops	6 country-style pork ribs
Marinade:	**Marinade:**
1 teaspoon mustard powder	1 teaspoon mustard powder
1 teaspoon salt	1 teaspoon salt
¼ to ½ teaspoon chilli powder to taste	¼ to ½ teaspoon chili powder to taste
1 tablespoon dark brown sugar	1 tablespoon firmly packed dark brown sugar
1 × 298 g/10½ oz can condensed tomato soup	1 × 10½ oz can condensed tomato soup
2 tablespoons vinegar	2 tablespoons vinegar
2 tablespoons Worcestershire sauce	2 tablespoons Worcestershire sauce
2 tablespoons soy sauce	2 tablespoons soy sauce

Place the meat in a shallow dish. In a bowl, mix all the remaining ingredients together and pour over the meat. Marinate for 1 to 2 hours. Remove the meat and reserve the marinade. Place the meat on a well-oiled barbecue grill over hot coals and cook for 10 minutes each side, basting with the remaining marinade.
Serves 6

Fruity Pork Kebabs

METRIC/IMPERIAL	AMERICAN
Baste:	**Baste:**
175 g/6 oz soft brown sugar	1 cut firmly packed light brown sugar
4 tablespoons apricot jam	4 tablespoons apricot jam
2 tablespoons Worcestershire sauce	2 tablespoons Worcestershire sauce
6 tablespoons vinegar	6 tablespoons vinegar
1 teaspoon dry mustard	1 teaspoon dry mustard
Kebabs:	**Kebabs:**
450 g/1 lb pork fillet, cut into 2.5 cm/1 inch cubes	1 lb pork tenderloin, cut into 1 inch cubes
1 × 227 g/8 oz can apricots, drained	1 × ½ lb can apricots, drained
8 prunes, soaked	8 prunes, soaked

Combine all the baste ingredients in a small saucepan and heat gently until the sugar dissolves. Arrange the pork, apricots and prunes alternately on 4 oiled skewers. Brush with the baste and cook over medium hot coals for 15 minutes, turning and basting frequently.
Serves 4

Poultry Dishes

Chicken, duck or turkey can be cooked over the coals, but always thaw frozen portions before barbecuing. Turn and baste frequently during cooking until golden. Always test by piercing the flesh with a skewer. When cooked the juices will run clear.

Chicken on the Spit

METRIC/IMPERIAL	AMERICAN
1 × 1.5 kg/3 lb oven-ready chicken	1 × 3 lb roasting chicken
salt	salt
freshly ground black pepper	freshly ground black pepper
100 g/4 oz butter, melted	½ cup melted butter

Wipe the chicken inside and out and sprinkle with salt and pepper. Truss the chicken firmly and insert the spit rod through the centre of the bird from the neck to the tail.

Place the rod in position over medium hot coals and cook for approximately 45 minutes or until the flesh is tender and the skin is golden brown. When cooked the drumsticks should feel tender and move easily. Baste the chicken frequently with the butter while cooking. Carve the bird and serve with salad.
Serves 4 to 6
Note:
Put the bird on the spit before starting the fire and turn it to make sure it is evenly balanced. For ease of cooking, the fire should be near the back of the barbecue with a drip pan in front, under the bird, to catch the juices. These juices can be used with butter for basting.

Chicken on the Spit

Orange-Glazed Chicken

METRIC/IMPERIAL	AMERICAN
4 chicken halves, skinned	4 chicken halves, skinned
salt	salt
freshly ground black pepper	freshly ground black pepper
Marinade and Glaze:	**Marinade and Glaze:**
4 tablespoons clear honey	4 tablespoons honey
juice of ½ lemon	juice of ½ lemon
grated rind of 1 orange	grated rind of 1 orange
juice of 2 oranges	juice of 2 oranges
2 tablespoons Worcestershire sauce	2 tablespoons Worcestershire sauce
1 tablespoon soy sauce	1 tablespoon soy sauce

Combine all the marinade ingredients in a saucepan and heat gently for 2 minutes. Allow to cool. Place the chicken in a shallow dish and pour over the marinade. Leave for 12 to 24 hours, turning occasionally. Remove chicken and reserve the marinade. Place the chicken in a roasting tin (pan) and cook in a preheated moderate oven (180°C/350°F, Gas Mark 4) for 1 hour.

When required, brush the chicken well with the reserved marinade and sprinkle with salt and pepper. Place on an oiled barbecue grill over medium hot coals. Cook for about 10 to 15 minutes. Brush with the marinade during cooking and turn the chicken frequently until well glazed and crisp. Serve with jacket potatoes.
Serves 2 to 4
Illustrated on page 39

Turkey Surprise

METRIC/IMPERIAL

450 g/1 lb turkey meat,
  minced
50 g/2 oz parsley and
  thyme stuffing mix
2 teaspoons
  Worcestershire
  sauce
grated rind of 1 lemon
1 egg, beaten
salt
freshly ground black
  pepper
100 g/4 oz cream
  cheese
1 teaspoon chopped
  sage
oil for brushing

AMERICAN

2 cups firmly packed
  ground turkey meat
½ cup parsley and
  thyme stuffing mix
2 teaspoons
  Worcestershire
  sauce
grated rind of 1 lemon
1 egg, beaten
salt
freshly ground black
  pepper
½ cup cream cheese
1 teaspoon chopped
  sage
oil for brushing

In a large bowl, mix the turkey, stuffing mix, Worcestershire sauce, lemon rind and egg. Sprinkle with salt and pepper. In another bowl mix the cheese and sage. Divide the turkey mixture into 8 and shape each piece into a flat patty. Place a quarter of the cheese mixture in the middle of 4 of the patties. Top each with one of the remaining patties, and press edges together firmly. Place on an oiled barbecue grill over medium hot coals and cook for about 10 minutes on each side, brushing lightly with oil during cooking.
Serves 4

Turkey Drummers

METRIC/IMPERIAL

50 g/2 oz butter
4 turkey drumsticks
1 onion, chopped
4 tablespoons tomato
  ketchup
2 tablespoons vinegar
2 tablespoons mango
  chutney, chopped
1 tablespoon
  Worcestershire
  sauce
½ teaspoon French
  mustard

AMERICAN

¼ cup butter
4 turkey drumsticks
1 onion, chopped
4 tablespoons ketchup
2 tablespoons vinegar
2 tablespoons mango
  chutney, chopped
1 tablespoon
  Worcestershire
  sauce
½ teaspoon Dijon-style
  mustard

Melt half the butter in a frying pan (skillet) and fry the drumsticks until brown all over. Cut 4 pieces of double aluminium foil and place one drumstick on each. Add the remaining butter to the pan and sauté the onion gently until soft, without browning. Add the remaining ingredients and bring to the boil. Spoon a quarter of the sauce over each drumstick. Seal the edges of the foil well to form individual parcels. Place on a barbecue grill over medium hot coals and cook for about 30 to 40 minutes, turning two or three times during cooking.
Serves 4

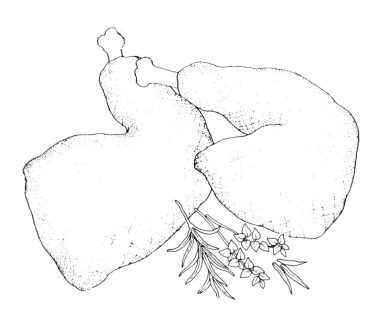

Herbed Chicken

METRIC/IMPERIAL	AMERICAN
4 chicken portions	4 chicken portions
200 ml/⅓ pint oil	⅞ cup oil
juice of 1 lemon	juice of 1 lemon
1 teaspoon chilli powder	1 teaspoon chili powder
2 cloves garlic, crushed	2 cloves garlic, crushed
generous pinch each of rosemary, oregano, tarragon and parsley	generous pinch each of rosemary, oregano, tarragon and parsley
salt	salt
freshly ground black pepper	freshly ground black pepper

Score the chicken skin with a sharp knife and place in a shallow dish. In a bowl, combine the oil, lemon juice, chilli powder, garlic, herbs and salt and pepper and pour over the chicken. Leave to marinate in the herb mixture for at least 4 hours.

Drain chicken and reserve marinade. Place the chicken on an oiled barbecue grill over medium hot coals. Cook for about 20 minutes. Turn and baste frequently with the marinade.
Serves 4
Illustrated on page 39

Patio Chicken

METRIC/IMPERIAL	AMERICAN
6 chicken joints	6 chicken joints
1 onion, finely chopped	1 onion, finely chopped
150 ml/¼ pint lime juice cordial	⅔ cup lime juice cordial
1 teaspoon chopped fresh tarragon	1 teaspoon chopped fresh tarragon
1 teaspoon salt	1 teaspoon salt
½ teaspoon Tabasco sauce	½ teaspoon hot pepper sauce

Wipe the chicken, pat dry on kitchen paper, and place in a shallow dish. Mix all the remaining ingredients in a bowl and pour over the chicken. Leave to marinate overnight. Drain the joints and reserve marinade. Place on an oiled barbecue grill over medium hot coals. Cook for about 15 to 20 minutes, brushing frequently with the marinade and turning once or twice during cooking.
Serves 6

Crispy Chicken with Mayonnaise

METRIC/IMPERIAL	AMERICAN
2 tablespoons Worcestershire sauce	2 tablespoons Worcestershire sauce
2 tablespoons sugar	2 tablespoons sugar
1 tablespoon tomato purée	1 tablespoon tomato paste
6 chicken or 3 turkey drumsticks	6 chicken or 3 turkey drumsticks
50 g/2 oz butter, melted	¼ cup melted butter
50 g/2 oz fresh white breadcrumbs	1 cup fresh, soft bread crumbs
25 g/1 oz walnuts, chopped	¼ cup chopped walnuts
Mayonnaise:	**Mayonnaise:**
150 ml/¼ pint mayonnaise	⅔ cup mayonnaise
3 tablespoons Worcestershire sauce	3 tablespoons Worcestershire sauce
2 tablespoons lemon juice	2 tablespoons lemon juice
3 tablespoons single cream	3 tablespoons light cream

In a small bowl, combine the Worcestershire sauce, sugar and tomato purée (paste). Place the drumsticks in a shallow dish and pour over the marinade. Cover and leave to marinate for 30 minutes.

Melt the butter in a saucepan, add the breadcrumbs and nuts, stir well and sauté until the crumbs are golden. Set aside.

Drain the drumsticks and reserve the marinade. Place on an oiled barbecue grill over medium hot coals. Cook for about 10 to 15 minutes, basting with the marinade and turning occasionally. Cool drumsticks slightly and coat in the fried crumbs.

Whisk all the mayonnaise ingredients in a small bowl and serve in the centre of a plate, surrounded by the drumsticks.
Serves 3 or 6

Tandoori Chicken

METRIC/IMPERIAL
1 teaspoon cayenne
  pepper
2 tablespoons lemon
  juice
salt
freshly ground black
  pepper
4 chicken portions,
  skinned
3 tablespoons melted
  butter
Marinade:
1 teaspoon powdered
  ginger
4 cloves garlic,
  crushed
1 teaspoon coriander
1 tablespoon cumin
  powder
2 tablespoons lemon
  juice
3 tablespoons plain
  yogurt
1 tablespoon cayenne
  pepper
1 teaspoon red food
  colouring

AMERICAN
1 teaspoon cayenne
2 tablespoons lemon
  juice
salt
freshly ground black
  pepper
4 chicken portions,
  skinned
3 tablespoons melted
  butter
Marinade:
1 teaspoon powdered
  ginger
4 cloves garlic,
  crushed
1 teaspoon coriander
1 tablespoon cumin
  powder
2 tablespoons lemon
  juice
3 tablespoons plain
  yogurt
1 tablespoon cayenne
1 teaspoon red food
  coloring

In a cup mix the cayenne, lemon juice, salt and pepper and rub over the chicken. Leave for 45 minutes. In a bowl, combine all the marinade ingredients. Place the chicken in a shallow dish and coat generously with the marinade.

Cover and refrigerate for at least 12 hours. Remove the chicken, drain and reserve marinade. Divide between 2 skewers. Place on a barbecue grill over medium hot coals and cook for about 20 to 25 minutes. Baste regularly with melted butter and remaining marinade during cooking to prevent the chicken from burning. Serve with a mixed salad.
Serves 4

Devil's Drumsticks

METRIC/IMPERIAL
8 chicken drumsticks
2 teaspoons salt
2 teaspoons sugar
1 teaspoon freshly
  ground black
  pepper
1 teaspoon ground
  ginger
1 teaspoon dry
  mustard
½ teaspoon curry
  powder
50 g/2 oz butter,
  melted
Sauce:
2 tablespoons tomato
  ketchup
1 tablespoon
  mushroom ketchup
1 tablespoon
  Worcestershire
  sauce
1 tablespoon soy
  sauce
4 drops Tabasco
  sauce
1 tablespoon plum
  jam

AMERICAN
8 chicken drumsticks
2 teaspoons salt
2 teaspoons sugar
1 teaspoon freshly
  ground black
  pepper
1 teaspoon ground
  ginger
1 teaspoon dry
  mustard
½ teaspoon curry
  powder
¼ cup melted butter
Sauce:
2 tablespoons ketchup
1 tablespoon
  mushroom ketchup
1 tablespoon
  Worcestershire
  sauce
1 tablespoon soy
  sauce
4 drops hot pepper
  sauce
1 tablespoon plum
  jam

Score the chicken skin with a sharp knife and place in a shallow dish. In a bowl, mix the salt, sugar, pepper, ginger, mustard and curry powder and dust the chicken completely with this mixture. Leave for 1 hour. Brush the chicken with the melted butter.

In a saucepan, mix the sauce ingredients. Heat gently. Place the chicken drumsticks on an oiled barbecue grill over medium hot coals. Cook for 10 to 15 minutes or until brown and crisp, basting continuously with the hot sauce.

Serve any remaining sauce with the chicken.
Serves 4 to 8

*Clockwise from the top—
Orange-Glazed Chicken (page 35), Herbed
Chicken, (page 37), Chicken Satay (page 40),
Devil's Drumsticks, Tasty Chicken Parcels
(page 41), Tandoori Chicken
(Photograph: British Chicken Information
Service)*

Spiced Chicken

METRIC/IMPERIAL	AMERICAN
8 chicken or 4 turkey drumsticks	8 chicken or 4 turkey drumsticks
Marinade:	**Marinade:**
1 tablespoon oil	1 tablespoon oil
1 onion, sliced	1 onion, sliced
1–2 cloves garlic, crushed	1–2 cloves garlic, crushed
1 teaspoon chilli powder	1 teaspoon chili powder
1 × 298 g/10½ oz can condensed cream of chicken soup	1 × 10½ oz can condensed cream of chicken soup
1 tablespoon mild curry powder	1 tablespoon mild curry powder

Place the drumsticks in a shallow dish. Heat the oil in a saucepan and gently sauté the onion until soft. Add the remaining ingredients and bring to the boil. Reduce heat and simmer for 5 minutes. Cool the marinade and pour over the drumsticks, cover and leave for at least 1 hour.

Drain the drumsticks and reserve marinade. Place on an oiled barbecue grill over medium hot coals. Cook for about 15 minutes, basting frequently with the marinade. Serve hot.
Serves 4 or 8

Chicken Satay

METRIC/IMPERIAL	AMERICAN
8 chicken wing joints	8 chicken wing joints
salt	salt
freshly ground black pepper	freshly ground black pepper
1 tablespoon ground almonds	1 tablespoon ground almonds
1 tablespoon powdered ginger	1 tablespoon powdered ginger
1 teaspoon coriander	1 teaspoon coriander
1 teaspoon turmeric	1 teaspoon turmeric
300 ml/½ pint coconut milk	1¼ cups coconut milk
1 teaspoon demerara sugar	1 teaspoon firmly packed brown sugar
Satay Sauce:	**Satay Sauce:**
2 onions, roughly chopped	2 onions, roughly chopped
100 g/4 oz roasted peanuts	¾ cup roasted peanuts
pinch chilli powder	pinch chili powder
2 tablespoons oil	2 tablespoons oil
150 ml/¼ pint water	⅔ cup water
1 teaspoon sugar	1 teaspoon sugar
1 tablespoon soy sauce	1 tablespoon soy sauce
juice of ½ lemon	juice of ½ lemon

Sprinkle the chicken with salt and pepper and place in a shallow dish. In a bowl, mix the almonds, ginger, coriander and turmeric and gradually add the coconut milk. Pour over the chicken and leave to marinate for about 2 hours.

Meanwhile, make the sauce. Place half the chopped onion in a blender or food processor. Add the peanuts and chilli powder and process until the mixture is reduced to a paste. Heat the oil in a saucepan, add the remaining onion and sauté until soft. Add the paste and cook, stirring, for 3 minutes. Gradually add the water, stirring all the time. Stir in the sugar and cook for 5 minutes. Add the soy sauce and lemon juice and stir. Keep hot.

Drain chicken and reserve the marinade. Sprinkle with the brown sugar and place on an oiled barbecue grill over medium hot coals for about 15 to 20 minutes until the chicken is brown and crisp. Turn frequently and baste with the marinade. Serve with the sauce.
Serves 8
Illustrated on page 39

Tasty Chicken Parcels

METRIC/IMPERIAL	AMERICAN
8 chicken drumsticks	8 chicken drumsticks
oil for brushing	oil for brushing
8 courgettes, cut in 1 cm/½ inch slices	8 zucchini, cut in ½ inch slices
4 cloves garlic, finely chopped	4 cloves garlic, finely chopped
salt	salt
freshly ground black pepper	freshly ground black pepper
1 tablespoon tomato purée	1 tablespoon tomato paste
1 teaspoon basil	1 teaspoon basil
2 teaspoons sugar	2 teaspoons sugar

Brush the drumsticks with oil and place on the barbecue grill over medium hot coals. Cook for 2 minutes each side. Put each drumstick in a square piece of double aluminium foil. Arrange courgettes (zucchini) around each drumstick. Scatter with the garlic, salt and pepper. Add a dab of tomato purée (paste) and sprinkle each with a little basil and sugar. Seal the edges of the foil well to form 8 individual parcels. Place on the barbecue grill over medium hot coals and cook for about 10 minutes on each side. Serve straight from the foil.
Serves 8
Illustrated on page 39

Barbecued Stuffed Chicken Breasts

METRIC/IMPERIAL	AMERICAN
40 g/1½ oz butter	3 tablespoons butter
1 small onion, peeled and finely chopped	1 small onion, peeled and finely chopped
100 g/4 oz brown or white rice, washed and dried	½ cup brown or white rice, washed and dried
1 teaspoon turmeric or ½ teaspoon saffron powder	1 teaspoon turmeric or ½ teaspoon saffron powder
1 bay leaf	1 bay leaf
3 cloves	3 cloves
2 cardamom pods	2 cardamom pods
salt	salt
300 ml/½ pint water	1¼ cups water
4 chicken breasts, boned	4 chicken breasts, boned

Melt the butter in a saucepan and fry the onion with the rice until the onion is transparent. Add the turmeric or saffron, bay leaf, cloves, cardamom and salt to taste. Stir in the water and bring to the boil. Simmer gently until the rice is tender and the water has been absorbed.

Put the chicken breasts between sheets of greaseproof paper and beat until thin. Place a little stuffing on each breast and roll up. Secure with a skewer. Cook over hot coals, turning once.
Serves 4

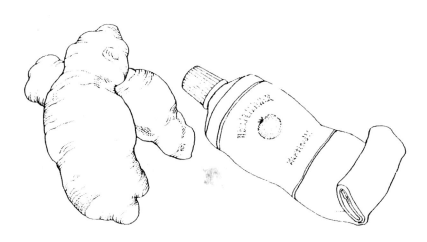

Fish Dishes

Whole fish, steaks, fillets and shellfish can all be barbecued successfully. Place the fish on a double layer of foil or use a double-sided hinged grill which holds the fish between two layers of mesh. While the fish is cooking, brush it with melted butter and lemon juice. Sprinkle with salt and freshly ground pepper before serving. Small fish can be threaded onto skewers for easy handling. Serve when the flesh flakes easily when tested with a fork.

Devilled Mackerel

METRIC/IMPERIAL	AMERICAN
4 mackerel, cleaned and with heads removed	4 mackerel, cleaned and with heads removed
100 g/4 oz button mushrooms, thinly sliced	1 cup sliced small mushrooms
Devilled Butter:	**Devilled Butter:**
50 g/2 oz butter, softened	$\frac{1}{4}$ cup softened butter
1 tablespoon Worcestershire sauce	1 tablespoon Worcestershire sauce
1 tablespoon dry mustard	1 tablespoon dry mustard

Wipe the inside and outside of the mackerel and lay each fish on a square piece of buttered double aluminium foil. Place a quarter of the mushrooms inside each fish. To make the devilled butter, mix all the ingredients in a small bowl. Place a quarter of the butter inside each fish, and seal the edges of the foil well to form individual parcels. Place on the barbecue grill over medium hot coals and cook for about 20 to 25 minutes, turning occasionally. Serve straight from the parcels.
Serves 4

Whole Fish Barbecue

Whole Fish Barbecue

METRIC/IMPERIAL	AMERICAN
1 × 1.5–2 kg/3–4 lb sea bass, bream or salmon trout, cleaned	1 × 3–4 lb sea bass, bream or salmon trout, cleaned
4 fresh fennel sprigs	4 fresh fennel sprigs
lemon wedges	lemon wedges
Wine Marinade:	**Wine Marinade:**
150 ml/$\frac{1}{4}$ pint white wine	$\frac{2}{3}$ cup white wine
2 tablespoons lemon juice	2 tablespoons lemon juice
1 onion, peeled and sliced	1 onion, peeled and sliced
1 carrot, peeled and sliced	1 carrot, peeled and sliced
1 stick celery, chopped	1 stalk celery, chopped
1 fresh parsley sprig	1 fresh parsley sprig
1 fresh thyme sprig or $\frac{1}{2}$ teaspoon dried thyme	1 fresh thyme sprig or $\frac{1}{2}$ teaspoon dried thyme
1 bay leaf	1 bay leaf
6 black peppercorns, slightly crushed	6 black peppercorns, slightly crushed
2–4 tablespoons oil	2–4 tablespoons oil

Mix together ingredients for marinade. Put the fish on a large double sheet of foil and fold up the sides. Pour over the marinade. Leave to marinate for 2 to 4 hours in the refrigerator. Put the fennel sprigs inside the fish and place the open foil parcel on the barbecue grid. Cook until the fish is tender, brushing with the marinade. Garnish with lemon.
Serves 6 to 8

Bacon Stuffed Trout

METRIC/IMPERIAL	AMERICAN
40 g/1½ oz butter	3 tablespoons butter
6 rashers of streaky bacon, chopped	6 bacon slices, chopped
1 onion, chopped	1 onion, chopped
100 g/4 oz mushrooms, sliced	1 cup sliced mushrooms
2 tablespoons chopped parsley	2 tablespoons chopped parsley
grated rind of ½ lemon	grated rind of ½ lemon
75–100 g/3–4 oz wholewheat breadcrumbs	1½–2 cups wholewheat bread crumbs
salt	salt
freshly ground black pepper	freshly ground black pepper
1 egg, beaten	1 egg, beaten
3 trout, cleaned	3 trout, cleaned

Melt half the butter in a frying pan (skillet), add the bacon and onion and sauté gently for 3 minutes. Stir in the mushrooms and continue cooking for a further 2 minutes. Tip the bacon mixture into a bowl and add the parsley, lemon rind and breadcrumbs. Mix well. Sprinkle with salt and pepper and bind with the egg. Place one-third of the stuffing in the cavity of each trout, closing the opening with fine skewers or cocktail sticks (toothpicks) if needed. Melt the remaining butter in a small saucepan and brush onto 3 square pieces of double aluminium foil. Place a fish in the centre of each piece of foil, brush with melted butter and sprinkle with salt and pepper. Seal the edges of the foil well to form individual parcels. Place on the barbecue grill over medium hot coals and cook for about 30 minutes or until the fish flakes easily when tested with a fork. Turn occasionally while cooking.
Serves 3

Spicy Herrings

METRIC/IMPERIAL	AMERICAN
4–6 herrings, cleaned	4–6 herrings, cleaned
3 small onions, quartered	3 small onions, quartered
4 tomatoes, halved	4 tomatoes, halved
salt	salt
freshly ground black pepper	freshly ground black pepper
Marinade:	**Marinade:**
300 ml/½ pint fish or chicken stock	1¼ cups fish or chicken stock
150 ml/¼ pint tomato ketchup	⅔ cup ketchup
2 tablespoons Worcestershire sauce	2 tablespoons Worcestershire sauce
2 tablespoons wine vinegar	2 tablespoons wine vinegar
2 tablespoons demerara sugar	2 tablespoons firmly packed brown sugar
2 drops Tabasco sauce	2 drops hot pepper sauce
2 tablespoons tomato purée	2 tablespoons tomato paste
1 tablespoon cornflour	1 tablespoon cornstarch

Cut the heads, fins and tails off the fish and cut each one in 4, crosswise. To make the marinade, mix all the ingredients except the cornflour (cornstarch) in a bowl. Place the fish in a shallow dish, pour the marinade over the fish, cover and leave for at least 1 hour.

Drain the fish, reserving the marinade, and thread onto oiled skewers, alternating with the onions and tomatoes. Sprinkle with salt and pepper. Place on the barbecue over medium hot coals and cook for about 10 minutes, basting with the marinade and turning frequently during cooking.

Blend the cornflour (cornstarch) with a little water to make a smooth paste. Add to the remaining marinade and pour into a saucepan. Heat until thickened, stirring constantly. Serve the fish on a bed of rice, accompanied by the sauce.
Serves 4 to 6

Herby Grilled Fish

METRIC/IMPERIAL	AMERICAN
4 whiting, trout or red or grey mullet, cleaned	4 whiting, trout or red or gray mullet, cleaned
salt	salt
freshly ground black pepper	freshly ground black pepper
1 teaspoon mixed herbs	1 teaspoon mixed herbs
2 sprigs of rosemary	2 sprigs of rosemary
4 tablespoons olive oil	4 tablespoons olive oil
1 tablespoon lemon juice	1 tablespoon lemon juice
1 teaspoon garlic purée	1 teaspoon garlic paste
lemon wedges to garnish	lemon wedges to garnish

Make 3 cuts across each side of the fish. Sprinkle with salt and pepper. Place the herbs in a shallow dish and lay the fish on top. Mix together the oil, lemon juice and garlic purée (paste) and pour over the fish. Cover and chill for 2 to 3 hours, turning several times. Drain fish and reserve marinade. Place the fish on an oiled barbecue grill over medium hot coals and cook for about 5 to 6 minutes each side, until cooked through and golden. Baste with the marinade during cooking. Serve garnished with lemon wedges.
Serves 4

Italian Fish Bake

METRIC/IMPERIAL	AMERICAN
25 g/1 oz butter	2 tablespoons butter
1 onion, sliced	1 onion, sliced
1 clove garlic, crushed	1 clove garlic, crushed
1 red pepper, cored, seeded and sliced	1 red pepper, cored, seeded and sliced
100 g/4 oz mushrooms, sliced	1 cup sliced mushrooms
1 teaspoon mixed herbs	1 teaspoon mixed herbs
4 whole red mullet or snappers, cleaned	4 whole red mullet or snappers, cleaned
salt	salt
freshly ground black pepper	freshly ground black pepper

Melt the butter in a saucepan, add the onion and garlic and sauté until soft. Add the pepper, mushrooms and herbs, mix well and continue cooking for 5 minutes.

Place each fish in the centre of a square piece of double aluminium foil and sprinkle with salt and pepper. Arrange a quarter of the vegetable mixture around each fish and seal the edges of the foil well to form individual parcels. Place on the barbecue grill over medium hot coals and cook for about 30 minutes, turning once during cooking. Serve in the foil.
Serves 4

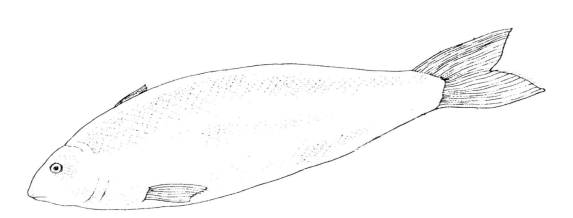

Prawns Poona

METRIC/IMPERIAL	AMERICAN
18 large Dublin Bay prawns, fresh or frozen	18 large Pacific prawns, fresh or frozen
6 tablespoons hot chutney	6 tablespoons hot chutney

Slit the prawn backs, de-vein and hinge open. Place them shell-side uppermost on an oiled barbecue grill, and cook for 3 minutes until pink. Turn over and place a little of the chutney in each prawn. Continue cooking for a further 5 minutes. Serve hot.
Serves 6 as an accompaniment
Illustrated on page 23

Halibut Steaks with Avocado

METRIC/IMPERIAL	AMERICAN
4 halibut steaks	4 halibut steaks
salt	salt
freshly ground black pepper	freshly ground black pepper
50 g/2 oz butter, melted	$\frac{1}{4}$ cup melted butter
1 tablespoon lemon juice	1 tablespoon lemon juice
1 teaspoon finely chopped chervil	1 teaspoon finely chopped chervil
Avocado Sauce:	**Avocado Sauce:**
1 ripe avocado, peeled and stoned	1 ripe avocado, peeled and seeded
3 tablespoons soured cream	3 tablespoons sour cream
1 teaspoon lemon juice	1 teaspoon lemon juice

Sprinkle the fish with salt and pepper. In a bowl, combine the butter, lemon juice and chervil and brush over the fish. If available, place the fish inside greased hinged grills and place on the barbecue grill over medium hot coals. Cook for about 10 to 15 minutes, turning frequently and basting with the flavoured butter during cooking.

Meanwhile, mash the avocado with a fork in a bowl and blend in the remaining ingredients. Place a spoonful of the mixture over each fish steak and serve immediately.
Serves 4

Baked Honey Mackerel

METRIC/IMPERIAL	AMERICAN
2 large mackerel, about 450 g/1 lb each, cleaned and with heads removed	2 large mackerel, about 1 lb each, cleaned and with heads removed
2 tablespoons clear honey	2 tablespoons honey
1 carrot, peeled and cut in 5 cm/2 inch julienne strips	1 carrot, peeled and cut in 2 inch julienne strips
1 stick celery, cleaned and cut in 5 cm/2 inch julienne strips	1 stalk celery, cleaned and cut in 2 inch julienne strips
1 piece ginger root, peeled and shredded	1 piece ginger root, peeled and shredded
salt	salt
freshly ground black pepper	freshly ground black pepper
1 tablespoon vinegar	1 tablespoon vinegar
1 tablespoon soy sauce	1 tablespoon soy sauce

Place each mackerel on a greased piece of double aluminium foil large enough to enclose the whole fish. Spread each fish with honey. Divide the carrot, celery and ginger root between the two. Add salt and pepper to taste and sprinkle a little vinegar and soy sauce over each fish. Seal the edges of the foil well to form 2 individual parcels. Place on the barbecue grill and cook over medium hot coals for about 20 minutes, turning once during cooking. Serve hot in the foil.
Serves 4

Baked Honey Mackerel
(Photograph: Gale's Honey Bureau)

Cod Flamenco

METRIC/IMPERIAL	AMERICAN
25 g/1 oz butter	2 tablespoons butter
1 tablespoon oil	1 tablespoon oil
1 onion, sliced	1 onion, sliced
225 g/8 oz green beans	$\frac{1}{2}$ lb green beans
2 tomatoes, skinned and sliced	2 tomatoes, peeled and sliced
2 tablespoons tomato purée	2 tablespoons tomato paste
1 green pepper, cored, seeded and sliced	1 green pepper, cored, seeded and sliced
salt	salt
freshly ground black pepper	freshly ground black pepper
4 × 225 g/8 oz cod steaks	4 × $\frac{1}{2}$ lb cod steaks

Melt the butter with the oil in a frying pan (skillet) and sauté the onion until soft. Add the beans, tomatoes, tomato purée (paste) and pepper and cook for a further 5 minutes. Sprinkle with salt and pepper. Place each cod steak in the centre of a square piece of greased double aluminium foil. Spoon a quarter of the vegetable mixture on top of each fish steak and seal the edges of the foil well to form 4 individual parcels.

Place on the barbecue grill over medium hot coals and cook for about 20 minutes.
Serves 4

Haddock and Gammon Skewers

METRIC/IMPERIAL	AMERICAN
3 gammon steaks	3 ham steaks
350 g/12 oz fresh haddock, skinned	$\frac{3}{4}$ lb fresh haddock, skinned
3 tablespoons olive oil	3 tablespoons olive oil
6 tablespoons white wine	6 tablespoons white wine
2 cloves garlic, crushed	2 cloves garlic, crushed
2 teaspoons chopped parsley	2 teaspoons chopped parsley
2 teaspoons chopped tarragon	2 teaspoons chopped tarragon
freshly ground black pepper	freshly ground black pepper

Place the gammon (ham) steaks in a saucepan. Cover with cold water and bring to the boil.

Reduce heat and simmer for 3 minutes. Drain and cool. Cut the gammon (ham) and haddock into cubes, and place in a shallow dish. In a bowl, mix the remaining ingredients together and pour over the meat and fish. Cover and leave for at least 2 hours in a cool place. Drain, reserving marinade. Thread the fish and gammon (ham) alternately onto 4 long oiled skewers. Place on the barbecue grill over medium hot coals and cook for 10 to 15 minutes, turning frequently and basting with the marinade.
Serves 4

Whiting with Almonds

METRIC/IMPERIAL	AMERICAN
4 whole whiting, cleaned	4 whole whiting, cleaned
25 g/1 oz plain flour	$\frac{1}{4}$ cup all-purpose flour
salt	salt
freshly ground black pepper	freshly ground black pepper
100 g/4 oz butter, melted	$\frac{1}{2}$ cup melted butter
50 g/2 oz flaked almonds, toasted	$\frac{1}{2}$ cup sliced almonds, toasted
juice of 1 lemon	juice of 1 lemon

Wipe and dry the fish. In a shallow dish, mix the flour and salt and pepper. Coat the fish evenly in the seasoned flour and, if available, place each one in a greased hinged grill. Place on the barbecue grill over medium hot coals and cook for about 20 minutes or until the fish flakes easily when tested with a fork.

Turn frequently during cooking, basting with a little of the melted butter. Mix the almonds and lemon juice with the remaining butter and pour over the cooked fish to serve.
Serves 4

Sardines with Horseradish Cream

METRIC/IMPERIAL	AMERICAN
12 fresh sardines, cleaned	12 fresh sardines, cleaned
Baste:	**Baste:**
2 tablespoons oil	2 tablespoons oil
1 tablespoon Worcestershire sauce	1 tablespoon Worcestershire sauce
1 tablespoon lemon juice	1 tablespoon lemon juice
salt	salt
freshly ground black pepper	freshly ground black pepper
Horseradish Cream:	**Horseradish Cream:**
150 ml/¼ pint thick mayonnaise	⅔ cup thick mayonnaise
1 tablespoon horseradish sauce	1 tablespoon creamy horseradish sauce
1 tablespoon chopped parsley	1 tablespoon chopped parsley

Wash and dry the sardines. Combine all the baste ingredients together in a bowl. Brush the fish with the baste, inside and out, and sprinkle with salt and pepper. Place on an oiled barbecue grill and cook for 8 to 10 minutes, turning once. Brush with the baste occasionally during cooking.

For the horseradish cream, combine all the ingredients in a bowl and serve with the barbecued fish.
Serves 4

Apple Mackerel

METRIC/IMPERIAL	AMERICAN
4 mackerel, cleaned and with heads removed	4 mackerel, cleaned and with heads removed
40 g/1½ oz butter	3 tablespoons butter
1 medium dessert apple, peeled, cored and diced	1 medium dessert apple, peeled, cored and diced
2 sticks celery, chopped	2 stalks celery, chopped
1 small onion, chopped	1 small onion, chopped
225 g/8 oz cooked long-grain rice	2 cups cooked long-grain rice
1 teaspoon lemon juice	1 teaspoon lemon juice
salt	salt
freshly ground black pepper	freshly ground black pepper

Wipe and dry the fish. Open the fish, press flat and lift out the backbone. Place each fish on the centre of a piece of greased double thickness aluminium foil.

Melt the butter in a frying pan (skillet) and sauté the apple, celery and onion until soft. Stir in the rice and lemon juice, sprinkle with salt and pepper and mix well. Use this mixture to stuff the mackerel.

Seal the edges of the foil well to form individual parcels. Place on the barbecue grill and cook for about 20 minutes, turning once during cooking. Serve hot.
Serves 4

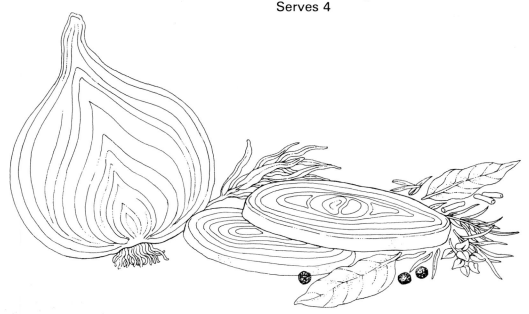

Side Dishes

Here is a selection of delicious accompaniments to your next barbecued meal. They are simple to prepare and serve. Select a vegetable, a salad and bread to complement your main dish.

Bacon Potatoes

METRIC/IMPERIAL
4 firm, even-sized
   potatoes
3–4 tablespoons oil
salt
freshly ground black
   pepper
225 g/8 oz streaky
   bacon, grilled until
   crisp, and chopped
4 tablespoons milk
To garnish:
4 rashers of streaky
   bacon
parsley or chopped
   chives
soured cream

AMERICAN
4 firm, even-sized
   potatoes
3–4 tablespoons oil
salt
freshly ground black
   pepper
½ lb bacon slices,
   grilled until crisp,
   and chopped
4 tablespoons milk
To garnish:
4 bacon slices
parsley or chopped
   chives
sour cream

Scrub the potatoes well, and dry. Prick with a fork, brush with oil and sprinkle with salt and pepper. Wrap each separately in a piece of aluminium foil. Place over hot coals or directly on the coals and cook for about 45 minutes to 1 hour. Turn occasionally while cooking.

Remove from the foil and slice off the tops. Scoop out the soft potato and place in a bowl. Add the chopped bacon, milk and salt and pepper, mix well and pile back into the skins. Wrap the foil around the potatoes again, and reheat for about 15 minutes.

Meanwhile prepare the garnish. Pleat the remaining bacon slices and push onto a skewer. Grill until crisp. Top each potato with a bacon slice, parsley or chives and sour cream.
Serves 4

Bacon Potatoes
(Photograph: British Bacon Bureau)

Variations:
Cheese-Stuffed Potatoes Mix together 75 g/ 3 oz/¾ cup grated Cheddar cheese, 1 tablespoon Worcestershire sauce, ½ teaspoon dry mustard, 3 spring onions (scallions) chopped, 50 g/2 oz/¼ cup butter and salt and pepper to taste. Combine with the soft potato scooped out of 4 baked potatoes and continue as for Bacon Potatoes. Reheat on the barbecue.
Savoury Baked Potatoes Mix together 225 g/ 8 oz/1 cup fresh shrimps (shelled and chopped), 3 tablespoons mayonnaise, salt and freshly ground black pepper and 100 g/4 oz/1 cup grated cheese. Combine with the soft potato scooped out of 4 baked potatoes and continue as for Bacon Potatoes. Reheat on the barbecue.

Aubergine Fans

METRIC/IMPERIAL	AMERICAN
2 × 350 g/12 oz aubergines	2 × 12 oz eggplant
2 firm ripe tomatoes, thinly sliced	2 firm ripe tomatoes, thinly sliced
1 clove garlic, finely chopped	1 clove garlic, finely chopped
1 onion, chopped	1 onion, chopped
4 canned artichoke hearts, quartered	4 canned artichoke hearts, quartered
2 tablespoons oil	2 tablespoons oil
12 black olives, stoned and sliced	12 black olives, pitted and sliced
½ teaspoon mixed herbs	½ teaspoon mixed herbs
salt	salt
freshly ground black pepper	freshly ground black pepper

Halve the aubergine (eggplant) lengthwise. Place the halves, cut side down, on a chopping board and slit each lengthwise at 1 cm/½ inch intervals, leaving the stem attached, to form a fan shape.

Place the tomato slices in the aubergine (eggplant) slits. Cut 4 pieces of double aluminium foil large enough to parcel each aubergine half. Reserve a little of the garlic and scatter remaining garlic with the onion over the bottom of each piece of foil. Arrange the aubergine halves on top. Coat the artichokes in 1 tablespoon of the oil and arrange them, together with the olives, in the 'fans'.

Brush each aubergine (eggplant) with the remaining oil and scatter the reserved garlic over the top. Sprinkle with mixed herbs and salt and pepper to taste. Seal the edges of the foil well to form individual parcels. Place on the barbecue grill over medium hot coals and cook for about 40 minutes or until the stem ends of the aubergine (eggplant) are soft.
Serves 4

Ratatouille

METRIC/IMPERIAL	AMERICAN
2 large courgettes, cut in 1 cm/½ inch slices	2 large zucchini, cut in ½ inch slices
1 large aubergine, cut in 1 cm/½ inch slices	1 large eggplant, cut in ½ inch slices
1 tablespoon salt	1 tablespoon salt
3 tablespoons oil	3 tablespoons oil
1 large onion, chopped	1 large onion, chopped
1 clove garlic, crushed with ½ teaspoon salt	1 clove garlic, crushed with ½ teaspoon salt
1 large green pepper, cored, seeded and sliced	1 large green pepper, cored, seeded and sliced
1 large red pepper, cored, seeded and sliced	1 large red pepper, cored, seeded and sliced
2 tablespoons Worcestershire sauce	2 tablespoons Worcestershire sauce
salt	salt
freshly ground black pepper	freshly ground black pepper
1 × 397 g/14 oz can tomatoes	1 × 14 oz can tomatoes

Place the courgettes (zucchini) and aubergine (eggplant) in a bowl, sprinkle with salt and leave covered for 1 hour to remove excess moisture.

Heat the oil in a large saucepan and gently sauté the onion and garlic for about 5 minutes until soft. Add peppers and continue to sauté for a further 5 minutes. Drain the courgettes (zucchini) and aubergine (eggplant) and wash well to remove excess salt. Add to the onion and pepper mixture. Stir in the remaining ingredients, cover and simmer for 30 minutes. Serve hot or cold.
Serves 4
Note:
Ratatouille can be made in advance and served cold as a salad.

Barbecued Sweetcorn

METRIC/IMPERIAL	AMERICAN
4 medium corn cobs	4 medium corn cobs
50 g/2 oz butter, melted	$\frac{1}{4}$ cup melted butter
salt	salt
freshly ground black pepper	freshly ground black pepper

Cut 4 pieces of double aluminium foil large enough to wrap around each corn cob. Brush the foil and the cobs with melted butter and place a cob in the centre of each piece of foil. Sprinkle each with salt and pepper. Seal the edges of the foil well to form individual parcels. Place on the barbecue grill over hot coals and cook for 20 to 30 minutes, turning frequently.
Serves 4

Note:
A slice of bacon can be wrapped around each corn cob before placing it in foil. The bacon helps to keep the corn moist and adds flavour during cooking. Cook for about 35 to 40 minutes or until the kernels are tender when pressed.

Stuffed Mushrooms

METRIC/IMPERIAL	AMERICAN
8 large mushrooms	8 large mushrooms
2 tablespoons fresh white breadcrumbs	2 tablespoons fresh white breadcrumbs
1 small onion, peeled and finely chopped	1 small onion, peeled and finely chopped
1 teaspoon mixed dried herbs	1 teaspoon mixed dried herbs
1 tomato, skinned and chopped	1 tomato, skinned and chopped
1 tablespoon oil	1 tablespoon oil

Remove the stalks from the mushrooms and chop finely. Mix the stalks with the breadcrumbs, onion, herbs and tomato. Brush the mushroom caps with oil and arrange on an oiled flameproof plate. Spread each cap with the stuffing and place on the barbecue grid to cook. Decorate with sprigs of parsley, strips of pimiento or tomato, if liked.
Serves 4

Naan (Baked Leavened Bread)

METRIC/IMPERIAL	AMERICAN
225 g/8 oz plain flour	2 cups all-purpose flour
$\frac{1}{2}$ teaspoon baking powder	$\frac{1}{2}$ teaspoon baking powder
1 teaspoon salt	1 teaspoon salt
1 teaspoon sugar	1 teaspoon sugar
1 teaspoon dried yeast	1 teaspoon active dry yeast
150 ml/$\frac{1}{4}$ pint milk	$\frac{2}{3}$ cup milk
150 ml/$\frac{1}{4}$ pint plain yogurt	$\frac{2}{3}$ cup plain yogurt
1 egg, beaten	1 egg, beaten
2 teaspoons poppy seeds (optional)	2 teaspoons poppy seeds (optional)

Sift the flour, baking powder, salt and sugar into a bowl. In a cup, mix the yeast to a paste with a little of the milk. Place the yogurt in a saucepan with the remaining milk and heat until lukewarm. Stir in the yeast paste. Add this mixture gradually to the flour and mix to a dough. Knead well, then add the egg and knead again. Cover the dough with a damp cloth and leave in a warm place for 1$\frac{1}{2}$ hours or until doubled in size.

Break the dough into 6 to 8 pieces, approximately 6 cm/2$\frac{1}{2}$ inches in diameter. Roll into balls and flatten with your hand. Dip your fingertips into the poppy seeds (if used) and press into the naan. Place on baking sheets and bake in a preheated hot oven (230°C/450°F, Gas Mark 8) for 12 minutes or until the naan are puffed and blistered. If not required immediately, wrap in aluminium foil and keep warm on the edge of the barbecue.
Makes 6 to 8
Illustrated on page 23

Filled French Bread

METRIC/IMPERIAL
1 French bread stick
450 g/1 lb cream
cheese, softened
1 tablespoon mixed
herbs
5 tablespoons
mayonnaise
1 × 113 g/4 oz jar
pimientos, drained
and chopped
2 tablespoons freshly
chopped parsley
salt
freshly ground black
pepper

AMERICAN
1 French bread stick
2 cups cream cheese,
softened
1 tablespoon mixed
herbs
5 tablespoons
mayonnaise
1 × ¼ lb jar pimientos,
drained and
chopped
2 tablespoons freshly
chopped parsley
salt
freshly ground black
pepper

Cut the bread crosswise into quarters. With a fork, hollow out the centre of each, leaving a 1 cm/½ inch shell. Mix the remaining ingredients in a bowl, with salt and pepper to taste. Pack the mixture into the bread quarters, wrap in foil and chill for at least 3 hours.
Makes 35 to 40 slices

Hot Garlic and Sausage Loaf

METRIC/IMPERIAL
1 small French bread
stick
50 g/2 oz butter,
softened
2 cloves garlic,
crushed
salt
freshly ground black
pepper
8 thin pork sausages
oil for brushing

AMERICAN
1 small French bread
stick
¼ cup softened butter
2 cloves garlic,
crushed
salt
freshly ground black
pepper
8 thin pork sausage
links
oil for brushing

Make 8 equally spaced cuts into the bread, almost through to the bottom. In a bowl, mix the butter and garlic. Add salt and pepper to taste and beat until smooth. Divide the mixture between the loaf slices. Wrap the loaf securely in aluminium foil and place on the barbecue grill over medium hot coals. Cook for about 15 minutes, turning once during cooking.

Meanwhile, brush the sausages with oil and place on the barbecue grill. Cook for about 10 minutes, turning occasionally. Unwrap the bread and place a sausage between each slice.
Serves 4

Cheese and Chive Bread

METRIC/IMPERIAL
225 g/8 oz plain flour
1 teaspoon salt
2 teaspoons dry
mustard
4 teaspoons baking
powder
225 g/8 oz
wholewheat flour
100 g/4 oz butter
225 g/8 oz cheese,
finely grated
1 onion, finely
chopped
1 tablespoon fresh
chives
2 eggs, lightly beaten
150 ml/¼ pint milk
1 egg, to glaze

AMERICAN
2 cups all-purpose
flour
1 teaspoon salt
2 teaspoons dry
mustard
4 teaspoons baking
powder
2 cups wholewheat
flour
½ cup butter
2 cups finely grated
cheese
1 onion, finely
chopped
1 tablespoon fresh
chives
2 eggs, lightly beaten
⅔ cup milk
1 egg, to glaze

In a mixing bowl, sift the plain (all-purpose) flour, salt, mustard and baking powder. Add the wholewheat flour and rub (cut) in the butter until the mixture resembles fine breadcrumbs. Add the cheese, onion and chives and mix well. Add the eggs and milk and mix to a soft dough.

Shape into a large round and score the top into 8 wedges. Transfer to a greased baking sheet and brush with the beaten egg. Place in a preheated moderately hot oven (190°C/375°F, Gas Mark 5) for about 1 hour, until well risen and golden brown.

Transfer to a wire cooling tray. Cut into wedges and serve buttered with hamburgers, sausages or other barbecued foods.
Makes 8 wedges

Cheese and Chive Bread
(Photograph: Dutch Dairy Bureau)

Hot Rice Salad

METRIC/IMPERIAL
Dressing:
3 tablespoons
    tarragon vinegar
salt
freshly ground black
    pepper
1 clove garlic, crushed
2 tablespoons capers
1 tablespoon chopped
    parsley
1 tablespoon chopped
    chives
1 tablespoon dry
    mustard
1 teaspoon sugar
4 tablespoons salad
    oil
Salad:
200 g/7 oz long-grain
    rice
600 ml/1 pint water
1 teaspoon salt
1 hard-boiled egg,
    chopped, to garnish

AMERICAN
Dressing:
3 tablespoons
    tarragon vinegar
salt
freshly ground black
    pepper
1 clove garlic, crushed
2 tablespoons capers
1 tablespoon chopped
    parsley
1 tablespoon chopped
    chives
1 tablespoon dry
    mustard
1 teaspoon sugar
4 tablespoons salad
    oil
Salad:
1 cup long-grain rice
2½ cups water
1 teaspoon salt
1 hard-cooked egg,
    chopped, to garnish

Mix the dressing ingredients in a screw-topped jar. Shake well.

Put the rice, water and salt into a saucepan. Bring to the boil and stir once. Lower the heat, cover and simmer for about 15 minutes or until the rice is tender and the liquid has been absorbed.

Mix the dressing into the warm cooked rice and serve garnished with the chopped egg. The rice can be kept warm at the side of the barbecue.
Serves 4

Peanut Potato Salad

METRIC/IMPERIAL
3 tablespoons
    crunchy peanut
    butter
1 tablespoon oil
1 tablespoon curry
    powder
1 teaspoon sugar
4 tablespoons water
450 g/1 lb potatoes,
    peeled, cooked and
    diced
To garnish:
1 red pepper, cored,
    seeded and diced
shredded lettuce
    leaves

AMERICAN
3 tablespoons
    crunchy peanut
    butter
1 tablespoon oil
1 tablespoon curry
    powder
1 teaspoon sugar
4 tablespoons water
3 cups diced cooked
    potato
To garnish:
1 red pepper, cored,
    seeded and diced
shredded lettuce
    leaves

In a bowl, mix the peanut butter, oil, curry powder, sugar and water. Stir well. Fold the diced potatoes into the peanut mixture and allow the salad to stand for about 2 hours before serving.

Garnish with the pepper and lettuce.
Serves 4 to 6

Tangy Cucumber Salad

METRIC/IMPERIAL
12.5 cm/5 inch length
    of cucumber, diced
½ small red pepper,
    cored, seeded and
    sliced
1 small orange,
    peeled and chopped
3 tablespoons
    mayonnaise
150 ml/¼ pint plain
    yogurt
shredded lettuce

AMERICAN
5 inch length of
    cucumber, diced
½ small red pepper,
    cored, seeded and
    sliced
1 small orange,
    peeled and chopped
3 tablespoons
    mayonnaise
⅔ cup plain yogurt
shredded lettuce

Mix the cucumber, pepper and orange in a salad bowl. In a bowl, mix the mayonnaise and yogurt and stir into the salad. Serve on a bed of shredded lettuce.
Serves 4

Artichoke Salad

METRIC/IMPERIAL
1 crisp lettuce
2 sticks celery, sliced
75 g/3 oz stuffed
  olives
1 × 397 g/14 oz can
  artichoke hearts,
  drained
2 tablespoons olive oil
1 tablespoon lemon
  juice
salt
freshly ground black
  pepper

AMERICAN
1 head crisp lettuce
2 stalks celery, sliced
3 oz stuffed olives
1 × 14 oz can artichoke
  hearts, drained
2 tablespoons olive oil
1 tablespoon lemon
  juice
salt
freshly ground black
  pepper

Wash the lettuce, drain and pat dry. Put into a plastic bag and refrigerate until crisp. Break the lettuce into pieces and place in a salad bowl with the celery and olives. Cut the artichoke hearts in half lengthwise and add to the lettuce.

In a screw-top jar, mix the oil, lemon juice, salt and pepper. Shake well. Just before serving, toss the salad with the dressing.
Serves 4 to 6

Honey-Lemon Slaw

METRIC/IMPERIAL
2 tablespoons
  mayonnaise
1 tablespoon honey
½ teaspoon grated
  lemon rind
1 tablespoon lemon
  juice
¼ teaspoon ground
  ginger
175 g/6 oz red
  cabbage, shredded
175 g/6 oz white
  cabbage, shredded
salt
freshly ground black
  pepper

AMERICAN
2 tablespoons
  mayonnaise
1 tablespoon honey
½ teaspoon grated
  lemon rind
1 tablespoon lemon
  juice
¼ teaspoon ground
  ginger
2¼ cups shredded red
  cabbage
2¼ cups shredded
  white cabbage
salt
freshly ground black
  pepper

In a large bowl, mix the mayonnaise, honey, lemon rind and juice, and ginger. Stir in the red and white cabbage and mix until evenly coated.

Sprinkle with salt and pepper to taste and serve chilled.
Serves 4 to 6

Tomato and Avocado Salad

METRIC/IMPERIAL
4 tomatoes, peeled
  and quartered
1 avocado
1 × 200 g/7 oz can red
  kidney beans,
  drained
Dressing:
4 tablespoons oil
2 tablespoons vinegar
1 teaspoon dry
  mustard
1 teaspoon sugar
2 teaspoons chopped
  fresh marjoram
salt
freshly ground black
  pepper

AMERICAN
4 tomatoes, peeled
  and quartered
1 avocado
1 × 7 oz can red
  kidney beans,
  drained
Dressing:
4 tablespoons oil
2 tablespoons vinegar
1 teaspoon dry
  mustard
1 teaspoon sugar
2 teaspoons chopped
  fresh marjoram
salt
freshly ground black
  pepper

First make the dressing, place all the ingredients in a screw-topped jar and shake well. Place the tomatoes in a bowl. Halve, stone, peel and slice the avocado and add it to the tomatoes with the drained beans. Pour the dressing over the salad and toss well.
Serves 4

Fennel salad

METRIC/IMPERIAL
175 g–225 g/6–8 oz
  courgettes, sliced
salt
1 large fennel, sliced
¼ cucumber, sliced
225 g French beans,
  sliced and cooked
6 stuffed green olives
Dressing:
150 ml/¼ pint soured
  cream
1 teaspoon mustard
  with seeds

AMERICAN
1 cup thinly sliced
  zucchini
salt
1 large fennel, sliced
1 cup thinly sliced
  cucumber
1 cup sliced French
  beans, cooked
6 stuffed green olives
Dressing:
⅔ cup sour cream
1 teaspoon mustard
  with seeds

Put the courgette (zucchini) slices on a plate, sprinkle with salt and leave for 15 minutes to draw out the excess moisture. Wash and thoroughly dry the courgette slices and place them in the bottom of a salad bowl. Place the thinly sliced fennel on top, then the cucumber and finally the beans.

Mix the soured cream with the mustard and pour it over the salad. Garnish with sliced olives, and chill for 30 minutes before serving.
Serves 4 to 6

Drinks & Desserts

To get your barbecue party off to a swinging start, serve ice cold Summer Citrus Cocktail when the weather is hot or Cider Mulled Punch on the cooler winter evenings. End with delicious desserts, either cooked on the barbecue or prepared in advance.

Summer Citrus Cocktail

METRIC/IMPERIAL
600 ml/1 pint fresh
  orange juice
600 ml/1 pint fresh
  grapefruit juice
600 ml/1 pint ginger
  ale
juice of $\frac{1}{2}$ lemon
crushed ice
To serve:
1 small orange, sliced
1 lemon, sliced
cocktail cherries
sprigs of mint

AMERICAN
2$\frac{1}{2}$ cups fresh orange
  juice
2$\frac{1}{2}$ cups fresh
  grapefruit juice
2$\frac{1}{2}$ cups ginger ale
juice of $\frac{1}{2}$ lemon
crushed ice
To serve:
1 small orange, sliced
1 lemon, sliced
cocktail cherries
sprigs of mint

Mix all the ingredients in a large jug. Add plenty of crushed ice and decorate with slices of orange, lemon, cocktail cherries and mint. Serve chilled.
Serves 6

Cider Mulled Punch

METRIC/IMPERIAL
2 litres/3$\frac{1}{2}$ pints dry
  cider
2 oranges, each stuck
  with 6 cloves
1 teaspoon ground
  cinnamon
2 dessert apples,
  cored and sliced
4 tablespoons sugar
4 tablespoons brandy

AMERICAN
9 cups hard cider
2 oranges, each stuck
  with 6 cloves
1 teaspoon ground
  cinnamon
2 dessert apples,
  cored and sliced
4 tablespoons sugar
4 tablespoons brandy

Pour the cider into a large saucepan and simmer for 5 minutes. Add the oranges, cinnamon, apple and sugar. Bring to the boil, stirring continuously, and stir in the brandy.

Using a slotted spoon, remove the oranges and take out the cloves. Slice the oranges thinly and return to the cider. Serve the warm mulled punch from the side of the barbecue.
Serves 12 to 15

Summer Citrus Cocktail
(Photograph: Summer Orange Office)

Party Cup

METRIC/IMPERIAL
1 bottle red wine
300 ml/½ pint port
150 ml/¼ pint brandy
150 ml/¼ pint orange juice
juice of 2 lemons
6 tablespoons sugar
grated rind of 1 lemon
grated rind of 1 orange
150 ml/¼ pint soda water
ice cubes
1 orange, thinly sliced, for decoration

AMERICAN
½ bottle red wine
1¼ cups port
⅔ cup brandy
⅔ cup orange juice
juice of 2 lemons
6 tablespoons sugar
grated rind of 1 lemon
grated rind of 1 orange
⅔ cup carbonated water
ice cubes
1 orange, thinly sliced, for decoration

Mix the wine, port, brandy, orange and lemon juice together in a large bowl. Stir in the sugar. Add the lemon and orange rind and soda (carbonated) water. Chill for about 30 minutes.

Add ice cubes and serve with the orange slices floating on top.
Serves 8 to 10

White Wine Sparkle

METRIC/IMPERIAL
1 bottle dry white wine
300 ml/½ pint lime juice cordial
4 tablespoons white rum
8 tablespoons dry Vermouth
1 × 227 g/8 oz can crushed pineapple
1 lime, sliced
1 lemon, sliced
5 cm/2 inch piece of cucumber, peeled and thinly sliced
900 ml/1½ pints lemonade
ice cubes

AMERICAN
1 bottle dry white wine
1¼ cups lime juice cordial
4 tablespoons white rum
8 tablespoons dry Vermouth
1 × 8 oz can crushed pineapple
1 lime, sliced
1 lemon, sliced
2 inch piece of cucumber, peeled and thinly sliced
4 cups lemonade
ice cubes

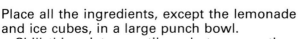

Place all the ingredients, except the lemonade and ice cubes, in a large punch bowl.

Chill this mixture until ready to serve, then add the lemonade and ice cubes. Stir well.
Serves 12

Cassata

METRIC/IMPERIAL
1.2 litres/2 pints vanilla ice cream
6 tablespoons finely chopped glacé fruits
2 tablespoons brandy
600 ml/1 pint chocolate ice cream, softened
50 g/2 oz flaked almonds, toasted
50 g/2 oz crushed macaroons
Decoration:
300 ml/½ pint double cream, whipped

AMERICAN
5 cups vanilla ice cream
6 tablespoons finely chopped candied fruits
2 tablespoons brandy
2½ cups chocolate ice cream, softened
½ cup sliced almonds, toasted
½ cup crushed macaroons
Decoration:
1¼ cups heavy cream, whipped

Line the bottom of a 20 cm/8 inch loose-bottomed cake tin (springform pan) with aluminium foil. Place half the vanilla ice cream in a bowl, and add the fruits and brandy. Spread the mixture over the base of the tin (pan) and freeze until very hard. Spread the chocolate ice cream over the vanilla layer and freeze again. Soften the remaining vanilla ice cream and spread over the chocolate layer. Press the almonds and macaroons lightly into the ice cream. Freeze for at least 30 minutes.

Turn out (unmold) and serve decorated with whipped cream.
Serves 8 to 10

Chocolate Refrigerator Cake

METRIC/IMPERIAL	AMERICAN
25 g/1 oz caster sugar	2 tablespoons sugar
1 egg	1 egg
225 g/8 oz plain chocolate, melted	8 squares semi-sweet chocolate, melted
225 g/8 oz unsalted butter, melted	1 cup melted butter
grated rind and juice of $\frac{1}{2}$ orange	grated rind and juice of $\frac{1}{2}$ orange
3 tablespoons brandy	3 tablespoons brandy
75 g/3 oz hazelnuts, chopped	$\frac{3}{4}$ cup chopped hazelnuts
225 g/8 oz digestive biscuits, broken	2 cups vanilla wafer crumbs
Decoration:	**Decoration:**
150 ml/$\frac{1}{4}$ pint double cream, whipped	$\frac{2}{3}$ cup heavy cream, whipped
$\frac{1}{2}$ orange, sliced	$\frac{1}{2}$ orange, sliced

Beat together the sugar and egg until light and frothy. Gradually add the chocolate and butter and fold in the remaining ingredients.

Pour into a lightly oiled 20 cm/8 inch round loose-bottomed cake tin (springform pan) and refrigerate until set. Remove from the tin (pan) and place on a serving plate. Decorate with piped whipped cream and slices of orange.
Makes one 20 cm/8 inch round cake

Crunchy Apple Layer

METRIC/IMPERIAL	AMERICAN
750 g/1$\frac{1}{2}$ lb cooking apples, peeled, cored and sliced	1$\frac{1}{2}$ lb tart apples, peeled, cored and sliced
75 g/3 oz sugar	6 tablespoons sugar
75 g/3 oz butter	6 tablespoons butter
100 g/4 oz fresh white breadcrumbs	2 cups fresh soft bread crumbs
To decorate:	**To decorate:**
150 ml/$\frac{1}{4}$ pint double cream, whipped	$\frac{2}{3}$ cup heavy cream, whipped
redcurrant jelly	red currant jelly

Place the apples in a saucepan and cook slowly with a third of the butter and just enough water to cover the bottom. When soft, mash the apples to a purée with a fork, adding 2 tablespoons of the sugar if the apples are very tart. Allow to cool.

Melt the remaining butter in a frying pan (skillet) and sauté breadcrumbs until golden. Stir in remaining sugar, and remove from the heat. Just before serving, arrange alternate layers of apples and crumbs in a glass bowl, finishing with a layer of crumbs. Decorate with the whipped cream and redcurrant jelly.
Serves 4

Mocha Hazelnut Ice Cream

METRIC/IMPERIAL	AMERICAN
2 teaspoons instant coffee powder	2 teaspoons instant coffee powder
1 tablespoon boiling water	1 tablespoon boiling water
150 ml/$\frac{1}{4}$ pint double cream	$\frac{2}{3}$ cup heavy cream
3 eggs, separated	3 eggs, separated
150 ml/$\frac{1}{4}$ pint plain yogurt	$\frac{2}{3}$ cup plain yogurt
50 g/2 oz hazelnuts, chopped in a blender	$\frac{1}{2}$ cup ground hazelnuts
50 g/2 oz plain chocolate, chopped	$\frac{1}{2}$ cup chopped semi-sweet chocolate
75 g/3 oz icing sugar	$\frac{3}{4}$ cup confectioner's sugar

Dissolve the coffee in the boiling water and leave to cool. Place the cream in a bowl and whisk until soft peaks form. Whisk in the egg yolks, one at a time. Fold in the yogurt, nuts and chocolate. Whisk the egg whites until very stiff then gradually whisk in the icing sugar. Fold the egg whites into the cream mixture then turn into a 1.5 litre/2$\frac{1}{2}$ pint (6 cup) freezer-proof container, cover and freeze until solid. There is no need to beat this ice cream during freezing.
Serves 6 to 8

Honeyed Bananas

METRIC/IMPERIAL	AMERICAN
8 under-ripe bananas	8 under-ripe bananas
25 g/1 oz butter, melted	2 tablespoons melted butter
4 tablespoons clear honey	4 tablespoons honey
2 tablespoons rum	2 tablespoons rum
1 tablespoon lemon juice	1 tablespoon lemon juice
To decorate:	**To decorate:**
50 g/2 oz flaked almonds	$\frac{1}{2}$ cup sliced almonds
150 ml/$\frac{1}{4}$ pint double cream, whipped	$\frac{2}{3}$ cup heavy cream, whipped

Peel the bananas and cut in half lengthwise. Cut 8 pieces of aluminium foil large enough to parcel each banana. Place 2 halves in the centre of each piece of foil. In a bowl, mix the remaining ingredients. Pour over the bananas. Seal the edges of the foil well to make 8 individual parcels and place on the barbecue grill over medium hot coals. Cook for about 10 to 15 minutes or until the banana is soft. Decorate with almonds and whipped cream.
Serves 8

Exotic Fruit Salad

METRIC/IMPERIAL	AMERICAN
1 large pineapple	1 large pineapple
75 g/3 oz dates, stoned and halved	$\frac{2}{3}$ cup pitted dates, halved
75 g/3 oz strawberries, halved	$\frac{2}{3}$ cup halved strawberries
2 kiwi fruit, peeled and sliced	2 kiwi fruit, peeled and sliced
few grapes, halved	few grapes, halved
1–2 tablespoons kirsch	1–2 tablespoons kirsch

Cut the pineapple in half lengthwise. Scoop out the centre to leave a thin 'shell'. Cut the pineapple flesh into neat pieces. Return to the shell with the remaining fruit and sprinkle with the kirsch. Chill for 1 to 2 hours before serving.
Serves 6 to 8
Note:
Mixed fruit on skewers makes a colourful dessert. Try threading pieces of banana, chunks of fresh pineapple, apple wedges, stoned (pitted) cherries and soaked prunes onto skewers.

Brush with a little honey, lemon juice and brown sugar and cook on a grill over medium hot coals for 5 minutes, turning frequently.

Spicy Oranges

METRIC/IMPERIAL	AMERICAN
4 large oranges, peeled and segmented	4 large oranges, peeled and segmented
50 g/2 oz demerara sugar	4 tablespoons firmly packed brown sugar
pinch of cinnamon	pinch of cinnamon
4 tablespoons rum	4 tablespoons rum
25 g/2 oz butter	$\frac{1}{4}$ cup butter
ice cream to serve	ice cream to serve

Cut 4 pieces of aluminium foil, large enough to parcel each orange. Place one segmented orange on the centre of each piece of foil. Turn the sides of the foil up, and sprinkle each with sugar, cinnamon and rum. Dot with butter.

Seal the edges of the foil well, to form 4 individual parcels, and place on the barbecue grill over medium hot coals. Cook for about 15 minutes, turning once during cooking. Remove the foil and serve with ice cream.
Serves 4
Note:
Apples are easily baked on the barbecue. Remove the cores and score each apple round the middle. Fill the cavities with sultanas (golden raisins) and brown sugar and top each with a knob of butter. Wrap each apple securely in foil and place on the grill over medium hot coals. Cook for about 45 minutes, turning once.
Serve with cream.

Index

The publishers would like to acknowledge the following photographers:
Bryce Atwell for the photographs on pages 26, 34 and 42; Paul Kemp
for the photograph on page 31. Illustrations by Lindsay Blow.